# Tending the
# Mustard Seed

# Tending the Mustard Seed

## Living the Faith in Today's World

by

Dennis J. Billy, C.Ss.R.

New City Press
of the Focolare
Hyde Park, New York

Published in the United States by New City Press
202 Comforter Blvd., Hyde Park, NY 12538
www.newcitypress.com
©2013  Dennis J. Billy

Cover design by Durva Correia


    Library of Congress Cataloging-in-Publication Data:

Billy, Dennis Joseph.
  Tending the mustard seed : living the faith in today's world / by Dennis J. Billy.
      p. cm.
  Summary: "Fr. Dennis Billy shares his personal experience of the call to faith
and its relationship to reason, prayer, suffering, healing, and community building.
Enriched by a wealth of references to scripture and Roman Catholic encyclicals,
each topic has an initial set of reflection questions and a meditative prayer"
"[summary]"--Provided by publisher.
  ISBN 978-1-56548-475-7 (alk. paper)
  1. Christian life--Catholic authors. 2. Faith. 3. Catholic Church--Doctrines. I.
Title.
  BX2350.3.B55 2012
  248.4'82--dc23
                            2012038050



Printed in the United States of America

For
Michael and Connie,
Richard and Phyllis,
Laura and Andy—
my brothers and sisters
in blood,
in law,
and in faith

# Contents

Abbreviations.................................................. 9

Introduction................................................... 13

Chapter 1: The Call of Faith ....................... 17

Chapter 2: The Gift of Faith...................... 28

Chapter 3: Faith and Reason...................... 37

Chapter 4: Faith and Prayer ....................... 49

Chapter 5: Faith and Suffering................... 59

Chapter 6: Faith and Healing..................... 70

Chapter 7: The Community of Faith......... 82

Conclusion: Living the Faith
    in Today's World.................................... 94

Acknowledgements.................................. 102

Notes........................................................ 103

# Abbreviations

AG   Second Vatican Council, *Decree on the Church's Missionary Activity (Ad Gentes,* 1965). English translation available at: http://www.vatican.va/archive/hist_councils/ii_vatican_council/documents/vat-ii_decree_19651207_ad-gentes_en.html

CD   Second Vatican Council, *Decree on the Bishops' Pastoral Office in the Church (Christus Dominus,* 1965). English translation available at: http://www.vatican.va/archive/hist_councils/ii_vatican_council/documents/vat-ii_decree_19651028_christus-dominus_en.html

DV   Second Vatican Council, *Dogmatic Constitution on Divine Revelation (Dei Verbum,* 1965). English translation available at: http://www.vatican.va/archive/hist_councils/ii_vatican_council/documents/vat-ii_const_19651118_dei-verbum_en.html

FR   John Paul, II, *Faith and Reason (Fides et Ratio,* 1998). English translation available at: http://www.vatican.va/edocs/eng0216/_index.html

GS   Second Vatican Council, Pastoral Constitution on the Church in the Modern World *(Gaudium et Spes,* 1965). English translation available at: http://www.vatican.va/archive/hist_councils/ii_vatican_council/documents/vat-ii_const_19651207_gaudium-et-spes_en.html

LG   Second Vatican Council, *Dogmatic Constitution on the Church (Lumen Gentium,* 1964). English translation available at: http://www.vatican.va/archive/hist_councils/ii_vatican_council/documents/vat-ii_const_19641121_lumen-gentium_en.html

PG   J. P. Migne, *Patrologia graeca*

PL   J. P. Migne, *Patrologia latina*

SC   Second Vatican Council, *Constitution on the Sacred Liturgy (Sacrosanctum Concilium,* 1963). English translation available at: http://www.vatican.va/archive/hist_councils/ii_vatican_council/documents/vat-ii_const_19631204_sacrosanctum-concilium_en.html

SCh   *Sources chrétiennes*

With what can we compare the kingdom of God, or what parable will we use for it? It is like a mustard seed, which, when sown upon the ground, is the smallest of all the seeds on earth; yet when it is sown it grows up and becomes the greatest of all shrubs, and puts forth large branches, so that the birds of the air can make nests in its shade.

*Mk 4:30–32*


If you have faith the size of a mustard seed, you will say to this mountain, "Move from here to there," and it will move; and nothing will be impossible for you.

*Mt 17:20*

# Introduction

Now faith is the assurance of things hoped for,
the conviction of things not seen.

*Heb 11:1*

Am I a person of faith? If so, what do I believe and how do I live it? Am I aware of my beliefs? Can I identify them? What do they mean to me? How does my daily life reflect them? Am I willing to act on them? Am I willing to die for them? What do I *truly* believe? What shapes my actions and gives meaning to my life?

Questions like these bring me face-to-face with my own difficulties of faith. The evidence is obvious enough. I say I believe in Jesus Christ, but often my thoughts and actions are shamefully shallow. I want to be his disciple, but often I am, at best, a reluctant follower with only skin-deep convictions. I wear a convenient mask of piety and play a convincing role, but when the going gets tough I drop everything and run away. I identify strongly with Peter, who denied Christ (Lk 22:54–62); Thomas, who doubted him (Jn 20:19–29); and Judas, who betrayed him (Mk 14:43–46). What they did I too often have done—and still do. I call myself a man of faith, but I realize how very, very weak my faith is. That fragile shoot sprouted from something much smaller than a mustard seed, and still needs careful tending.

In one parable, Jesus likens the kingdom of God to a tiny mustard seed that grows into the mightiest of shrubs with large branches in whose shade the birds of the air can nest (Mk 4:30–32). Elsewhere, he uses the image of the mustard seed to emphasize that his disciples' faith, as small as it is, has the power to uproot trees and move mountains (Lk 17:5–6; Mt 17:20). These tiniest of seeds illustrate the vital

connection between faith, however small, in the lives of his
followers and the growth of God's kingdom. The kingdom
of God thrives on the faith of its inhabitants. Belief in God,
even the smallest trace of it, has the power to work wonders.

I find it comforting that those whom Jesus called to
follow him had foibles similar to my own. His disciples
were flawed individuals whom their Master often chided
for their lack of faith. Yet with this carefully chosen group,
however imperfect, he established a kingdom of faith that
would spread to every corner of the earth. The words of the
fathers of the Second Vatican Council ring true:

> The joys and the hopes, the griefs and the
> anxieties of the men of this age, especially those
> who are poor or in any way afflicted, these are
> the joys and hopes, the griefs and anxieties
> of the followers of Christ. Indeed, nothing
> genuinely human fails to raise an echo in their
> hearts. For theirs is a community composed of
> men. United in Christ, they are led by the Holy
> Spirit in their journey to the Kingdom of their
> Father and they have welcomed the news of
> salvation which is meant for every man. That
> is why this community realizes that it is truly
> linked with mankind and its history by the
> deepest of bonds. (*GS 1*)[1]

This book is about faith: our need for it, our yearning for
it, our lack of it, and our hope for it. Faith is a multifaceted
reality demanding intellectual assent, personal trust, and
selfless, life-giving action. The author of the *Letter to the
Hebrews* describes it as "the assurance of things hoped for,
the conviction of things not seen" (Heb 11:1). Christians
hope for the fullness of life because of the passion, death,
and resurrection of Jesus Christ. Through faith, they receive
a foretaste of this new life in Christ and await its completion
in the world to come. Although this fullness cannot be
experienced in the present life, our faith assures us that it is

coming and deepens our conviction about the existence of another world, one not visible to the naked eye. "We walk by faith, not by sight," St. Paul says in his *Second Letter to the Corinthians* (2 Cor 5:7). Christians believe in the promises of God made visible in the person of Jesus of Nazareth, trusting that, through him, they will be fulfilled.

This book contains seven chapters. Chapter One, "The Call of Faith," considers faith as a response to an invitation from Jesus of Nazareth. When he walked this earth, Jesus chose certain individuals as his disciples; in the present age he extends this same call to everyone. Chapter Two, "The Gift of Faith," views faith not as a work dependent on human effort but as a gift from God that brings about a radical change of mind and heart. Chapter Three, "Faith and Reason," points out that faith is not a blind embrace of the absurd, but a recognition of the human limits to understanding the mystery of life. Faith does not contradict reason, but complements and even fulfills it. Chapter Four, "Faith and Prayer," presents faith as a seed in need of careful tending. Prayer is the life-giving water that nourishes the gift received at baptism, allowing it to grow and mature. Chapter Five, "Faith and Suffering," explains how through faith people find meaning in their suffering. Without faith suffering has no aim or purpose; with faith those who suffer gain perspective and connect their experience with a larger narrative of life. Chapter Six, "Faith and Healing," focuses on the curative aspects of faith on all levels: the physical, the emotional, the intellectual, the spiritual, and the communal. Belief in the resurrection points to the fullness of life in all areas of human experience. Chapter Seven, "The Community of Faith," examines how faith in Christ sustains the community and those belonging to it. Communion is essential to faith. While faith calls Christians into community with fellow believers and with all humanity, life in community deepens faith and helps to continue Christ's work on earth. The conclusion, "Living the Faith in Today's World," critiques the secular world's desire to squeeze faith out of life and life out of faith. Christians must engage human society without compromising their core values so as to share in the Spirit's work of a new evangelization. Throughout the book faith experiences taken from real life are set off as boxed texts. These biographical and autobiographical anecdotes illustrate and extend each chapter's theme.

Taken together, these chapters present a multifaceted approach to faith rooted deeply in the person of Jesus and his body, the Church. Although their scope and content do not exhaust the mystery of faith, they do identify the importance of faith in Christ in the life of every believer. To help in probing the mystery of faith in Christian life still further, each chapter ends with a series of reflection questions and a heartfelt prayer. By reflecting on faith and asking God to deepen it, believers become strong, faithful followers of Christ.

This book demonstrates how to tend the mustard seed of faith that God has planted in the soil of each believer's soul. People of faith quietly till the soil around that little plant, uproot the weeds of unbelief that would otherwise choke and kill it, water it with heartfelt prayer, and allow the sunshine of divine grace to fall upon it. With faithful cultivation, this tiny seed will send its roots deep into the ground of the soul and sprout upwards toward the radiant Sun. Over time, it will grow to maturity, spreading its branches to shelter others and to produce abundant fruit that gives flavor and spice to life. That is how Christians build the kingdom of faith where they live and help others do the same. All God asks is that they tend the tiny seed of faith planted deep within their souls—and leave the rest to him.

# 1

# The Call of Faith

As Jesus passed along the Sea of Galilee, he saw
Simon and his brother Andrew casting a net
into the lake—for they were fishermen. And
Jesus said to them, "Follow me and I will make
you fish for people." And immediately they left
their nets and followed him. As he went a little
farther, he saw James son of Zebedee and his
brother John, who were in their boat mending
the nets. Immediately he called them; and they
left their father Zebedee in the boat with the
hired men, and followed him.

*Mk 1:16–20*

F aith can be examined from various perspectives.
Scholars have investigated its content, dynamics,
stages, and various models. They have looked at
its roots in the natural order and its origins in the
supernatural. They have studied the act of faith, its object,
purpose, and the circumstances from which it arose. They
have even analyzed its relationship to human culture and
the human capacity to transcend it.[2]

Despite their many perspectives, scholars' conclusions
depend upon their tools of interpretation and their
assumptions. Materialists see faith as an escape from the
real world. Scientists, who often limit truth only to what can
be verified empirically, resist fitting faith into their world
view. Rational theorizing about the nature of existence
leaves philosophers little room for faith. Sociologists, in
turn, examine faith only inasmuch as it demonstrates
generational differences and societal trends, while political

pundits look to the voting records of faith groups and their impact on elections.

Such approaches to faith have value, but in some respect, all are lacking. Even Christian thinkers like me come up short in their explanations—and this study is no exception. My approach to faith has been shaped by my own experience; even my best efforts will capture only a small part of the reality of faith and its mysterious connection with the human spirit. For me, faith begins and ends with the experience of a call—and that is where I must begin.

## Like a Little Child

Jesus said that unless we become like little children we shall not enter the kingdom of heaven (Mt 18:3). Although I cannot recall the event itself, the seed of faith was planted deep in my heart when I was a little over a month old, on the day of my baptism. A picture of that moment in October of 1953 shows my godparents holding me over the baptismal font as the priest poured water over my head, pronouncing "In the name of the Father, and of the Son, and of the Holy Spirit." My expression reveals a mixture of peace and discomfort, probably from the cool water waking me up on that early Sunday afternoon. That photograph makes me consider how at that moment my soul too was waking up from a deep slumber.

On the day of my baptism, I was steeped in the waters of Christ's paschal mystery, immersed in the waters of his passion, death, and resurrection. On that day my old self was buried with Christ and a new self, symbolized by my white garments and my being anointed with oil under the light of the Paschal candle, took its place. It was the day of my second birth, when I became a member of Christ's mystical body, the Church. Although I have no memory of that day, the sacrament nevertheless left an indelible mark on my subconscious and on my soul. From that day forward, I was a child of God, a member of a large extended spiritual family, both visible and invisible, that over the centuries has spread throughout the world, bridging heaven to earth. It was the day when the Holy Spirit sanctified me and bestowed on me divine gifts. It was the day when my spirit first cried out "Abba, Father" (Rom 8:15), and when God entrusted me to my parents, godparents, family and larger faith community as a newborn child of faith, giving them responsibility to nurture my faith and help it grow to maturity.

Through the years, the tiny seed planted deep within my heart on the day of my baptism would eventually swell, break through the ground of my spirit, and sprout. What was once an unconscious movement of grace gradually rose to the surface of my awareness. In quiet moments, I could hear the Spirit moving among the newly formed branches and leaves of a young sapling, a sign that faith was alive and well within my soul. Within this small rustling sound was something more than a solitary, lonely ache. It was a groaning for wholeness, something more than this transitory world could give. It was a yearning for transcendence, a desire to go where I truly belonged. This quiet, whispering sound was within me, but came from beyond me. As I listened, I felt as though it were calling me to a place beyond space and time. It was calling me to holiness. It was calling me to engage with this world yet at all times to look beyond it. Most of all, it was a call to intimacy. Through the still small voice of his Spirit, Jesus himself was calling me, asking me to follow him as a disciple.

## Our Ancestors in Faith

The Scriptures are full of instances when God calls people to a life of faith. In the Old Testament, the Lord asks Abraham to leave his homeland for a land of milk and honey, and as a sign of his fidelity, to sacrifice his son Isaac

(Gn 12:1–9; 22:1–19). He asks Moses to lead his people out of Egypt (Ex 13:17–22), and appoints Joshua to lead them into the Promised Land (Jos 1:1–5). The prophet Samuel responds to God's call with a heartfelt "Speak, Lord, your servant is listening" (1 Sm 3:10). At Mount Horeb, Elijah hears the Lord not in a mighty wind, or earthquake, or fire, but in the sheer silence (1 Kgs 19:9–21). The Lord calls Isaiah and purifies his mouth with a fiery coal (Is 6:6–9); Jeremiah is told that he was appointed for his prophetic mission before being formed in his mother's womb (Jer 1:4–5). In the New Testament, Mary responds with her humble "Fiat" when asked to become the mother of the Lord (Lk 1:38). Four simple fishermen—Simon, Andrew, James and John—drop their nets and leave everything to follow Jesus (Mk 1:16–20). Levi, the tax collector gets up at once from his post at the customs house when Jesus asks that he follow him (Mk 2:13–14). On the road to Damascus, Saul falls off his horse and loses his sight when he hears the Lord's voice (Acts 9: 1–19). This is just a brief sample of those who have gone before us in faith. In each of these instances, God selects certain individuals to love and serve him on behalf of his people. Although they come from a variety of backgrounds, each has faith in the Lord's word and seeks to carry out his commands.

Responding to God's call, however, is not easy. All of these Biblical figures suffer for the words they speak and the actions they perform on the Lord's behalf. Abraham and his family undergo famine and must flee to Egypt (Gn 12:10–20). Moses and his people wander in the desert for forty years (Nm 32:13). Joshua must conquer the people who inhabit the land of Canaan (Jos 24:1–13). Samuel, disappointed that his sons cannot carry on his work, must anoint Saul as king (1 Kgs 8–12). Elijah flees from Queen Jezebel after he puts the prophets of Baal to the sword on Mount Carmel (1 Kgs 18–19). Isaiah suffers the heart-rending pain of having to announce the fall of Israel and

Judah, God's punishment for the nation's unfaithfulness (Is 1–12). Jeremiah announces a new covenant but is thrown down a cistern, barely escaping death (Jer 31:31–34; 38:1–13). Mary is overcome with sorrow as she witnesses the suffering and death of her son (Lk 2:33–35). The apostles suffer hardship for their faith in the Risen Lord; like Simon Peter, all but one meet a martyr's death (Jn 21:18–19). Paul is imprisoned, lashed, beaten with sticks, stoned, shipwrecked and set adrift in the open sea, and in Rome is eventually beheaded—all for the sake of the gospel (2 Cor 11:23–26). These ancestors in faith and members of the vast spiritual communion to which we belong believe in God's promises and suffer for their convictions.

## A Living Faith

Jesus said that the God of Abraham, Isaac and Jacob was not God of the dead, but of the living (Mt 22:32). We can learn a great deal from this "great cloud of witnesses" (Heb 12:1) who have gone before us.

These saints show how God knows each of us by name: "Before I formed you in the womb I knew you" (Jer 1:5). With these words the Lord reminds Jeremiah—and us—that the call of faith is intimately personal. God calls each of us to a special relationship of love with him and to manifest this love in our everyday relationships. Each of us, moreover, has a special calling. For some, it may be the priesthood or religious life. For others, it may be marriage and family. For still others, it may be a single life dedicated to a special work for the good of humanity, or being a friend to those in need and a support for those with no one to lean on. Each person knows, loves and serves God in a way no one else can. Most will discover the full reason why God has put them on this earth only when they see him face-to-face. In the meantime, God asks us to trust in his promises by following the example of Jesus, his son, who walked among us in order to befriend us, teach us, and show us the way home to the Father.

It is important that each person listen for God's call. In the past, God spoke through dreams, visions, and external signs. Today, he is more likely to speak in the deepest recesses of our hearts: "Speak, for your servant is listening" (1 Sm 3:11). These words of the prophet Samuel remind us that God speaks from heart to heart. To understand what he is saying, however, we must be comfortable with the backdrop of silence against which everything in our lives unfolds. Hearing his call requires a quiet, prayerful, listening heart so that, like the prophet Elijah, we may hear him in "the sheer silence" (1 Kgs 19:11). We must look upon this silence not as a threat, but as a friend. Because we can be mistaken in discerning God's will, we must also seek the opinion of devoted friends and sound spiritual counsel from trusted advisors. Responding to the call of faith requires taking time to discern its significance for our lives.

Even those with a listening and discerning heart may have difficulty understanding what God is saying. "We walk by faith, not by sight" (2 Cor 5:7). These words of St. Paul remind us that we seldom have absolute certainty when responding to God's call. Although guideposts can help in our discernment (e.g., Scripture, tradition, Church teaching), sometimes even these do not make clear the path we are being asked to follow. The call of faith often makes us move into the unknown. Just as Abraham left his homeland for an uncertain future, so we are called to let go of our familiar surroundings and trust that the Lord himself will guide us. When Jesus' first disciples dropped everything to follow him, they had no idea what the future would hold.

God sometimes strengthens our faith by allowing trials. For no clear reason, we may suffer intense physical, psychological, or spiritual pain. "Naked I came from my mother's womb, and naked shall I return there; the Lord gave, and the Lord has taken away; blessed be the name of the Lord" (Jb 1:21).

## Acting Upon Our Call

I was a girl who had it all — a beautiful family with lots of brothers and sisters to share life's every adventure and parents who have always been a shining example of how to overcome life's trials with faith and simplicity. I had a successful job, a new car, and a beautiful relationship with the guy I felt I would spend the rest of my life with. At the same time, I had a deep sense within me that this could not be everything in life. I was strongly attracted by a presence that I felt when I was with those who lived in the house of a nearby lay community. I would go there as often as I could for meetings or just to wash dishes, or put some shelves in order; anything to be there. Only later did I understand that the basis of this life was the commandment that Jesus called "new" and "mine": love one another as I have loved you. Living these words of the Gospel created an incredible atmosphere of Jesus' very presence in that house.

I was also attracted by how [my friends] lived a communion of goods, just like the first Christians. No one asked anything of me, but I began filling the trunk of my car once or twice a month with all that I no longer needed....

And I still felt urged inside to "give." It was at this point that I began to realize that more than my house, my money, my stuff, God wanted me.... For the little I have given, God is never outdone in generosity. Like the day that my brother said his first Mass in our tiny home town, he told me that I had been the one who, like a mother, generated his "yes." Or, years later, when I ran into my ex-boyfriend he said that my faithfulness had given him the strength to remain faithful to his own choices in life.[3]

These words come from someone whose faith in God is put to the severest of tests—Job. Despite losing his wealth, his family, and finally his health (Jb 1:1–2:12), he refuses to relinquish his faith. Eventually his steadfast trust is rewarded (Jb 42:10–17). Although Job questions his faith, he comes to accept that God's wisdom is beyond his understanding; he must simply trust in the Lord and hope to not be abandoned in his misery (Jb 42:1–6). We too sometimes bear heart-rending hardships and do not always understand why. Such times test the mettle of our faith and ask us to trust God even when we seem to have been abandoned.

Jesus' cry from the cross, "My God, my God, why have you forsaken me?" (Mt 27:46), presents the ultimate test of faith. Jesus, "the pioneer and perfecter of our faith" (Heb 12:2), offers the model par excellence of what it means to trust in God at all times, even at the moment of death. Jesus illuminates the path of faith for us, but even more he embodies it. He is "the way, the truth, and the life" (Jn 16:6). Without him, we are lost in the dark and cannot find our way. All of his disciples—Mary, his mother; Simon, Andrew, James and John, his first disciples; Paul, the great missionary to the Gentiles; and countless others—looked to him to understand what it means to trust in the Father's providential and benevolent love. His life, death, and resurrection remind us that intimacy with the Father comes only through intimacy with Jesus.

Finally, the call of faith is a call to follow Jesus: "If any want to become my followers, let them deny themselves and take up their cross and follow me" (Mk 8:34). The cross of Christ divides human history between those who anticipated it and those who look back to it. It proclaims the truth which was "a stumbling-block to Jews and foolishness to Gentiles" (1 Cor 1:23). The faith of our ancestors, that "great cloud of witnesses," reached its perfection in Jesus and lives on through his people, the members of his body, the Church. In this light, each person's faith is not an exclusive possession but a gift entrusted to the People of God: faith is both personal and communal. These two dimensions complement each other like the faces of a coin. Personal faith takes shape in the life of community, which in turn is enriched by the faith of its individual members.

These are but a few of the insights left by those who have gone before us in faith. This legacy contains an invitation and a challenge. God invites us to carry on the work of redemption by challenging us to follow the way of the Lord Jesus as members of his body, the Church. As stated in *Lumen Gentium*, "Just as Christ carried out the work of redemption in poverty and persecution, so the Church is called to follow the same route that it might communicate the fruits of salvation to men" (LG 8).

## Conclusion

The call of faith asks us to listen to our hearts and respond accordingly. It is a gift that God entrusts to us as individuals and as a people. It asks for our total commitment in the face of hardship, suffering and uncertainty. It leads to the feet of Jesus and the life of discipleship. It asks us to let go of ourselves so that we might find ourselves.

Jesus calls us to a living faith that rejoices in his presence in our midst and in our hearts. Like us in all things but sin (Heb 4:15), he stands at our side, helping us face whatever happens calmly, resolutely, joyously. He measures success not in terms of our honors, wealth, or power, but by our faithfulness to the Father, whom he loves and serves. As with the Old and New Testament saints, the call to faith sheds light on the path before us, helping us travel the highways and byways of life. Jesus extends this invitation to all men and women of good will and leads us to attain our destination in life and take it through death to the world beyond.

Faith is a call to intimacy with the divine. Jesus calls us as adopted sons and daughters of his Father in heaven to share in his divine Sonship (Eph 1:5). God loves us so much that he shares with us, the pinnacle of his creation, the love of his divine nature. St. Athanasius expresses this astounding reality best: "God became man so that man might become divine."[4] Faith leads us along the path of transformation, toward becoming more than we ever thought possible. It leads us along the road of sanctity, to a place where we are fully alive for the love of God.

## Reflection Questions

✧ With which of the Biblical figures cited in this chapter do you identify the most? What do you admire most about this figure? How does his or her call to faith resemble yours?

✧ How would you describe your own call to faith?

✧ When have you found it difficult to listen to God's voice? Do you find it difficult to listen to him now?

✧ Where does faith in God fit into the narrative of your life? How aware are you of that faith?

✧ What seems to be your special task in life?

## Living Faith

Lord, help me to be still and rest in your presence. Help me to listen to your voice in the quiet of my heart. Help me to hear what you are saying and discern the significance of your words for my life. Let me be open to whatever you have in store for me. Help me to seek your will in all things. Enable me to follow you in good times as well as bad, and to trust you at all times. Deepen my faith in you, Lord. Let me not hold anything back from you, and help me to call on you always, especially in my hour of need. *Mary, Mother of faith, pray for me.*

# 2

# The Gift of Faith

When they saw that the star had stopped, they
were overwhelmed with joy. On entering the
house, they saw the child with Mary his mother;
and they knelt down and paid him homage.
Then, opening their treasure-chests, they
offered him gifts of gold, frankincense, and
myrrh. And having been warned in a dream
not to return to Herod, they left for their own
country by another road.

*Mt 2:10–12*

Much of life is about giving and receiving gifts.
Children look forward to their birthdays and
Christmas with anticipation because of the
presents. It is special to receive a wrapped
present, to wonder what is inside, tear it open and discover
its secret. No matter our age, opening a gift brings out our
inner child. One of my earliest recollections of such an
event was receiving a toy trumpet for Christmas when I was
just six years old. It was new and shiny, something I could
call my very own. I was proud of myself as I learned to play
simple tunes and share them with my family and then with
my teacher and classmates when I brought it for show-and-
tell. That gift, something that I really wanted, made me feel
special. Thoughtful, heartfelt gifts do that. The gift of faith
does the same, and more.

## Giving and Receiving

One of my favorite stories about the art of giving and
receiving is O. Henry's "The Gift of the Magi."[5] In this tale,

a romantic young couple in early twentieth-century New York City struggle to find money to buy each other a special Christmas gift. With only $1.87 in savings for the year, Della cuts her long chestnut hair and sells it for $20.00, with which she buys a platinum fob and chain for her husband's gold watch. Without knowing what she has done, Jim sells his watch, a family heirloom, in order to buy an expensive set of combs for his wife's beautiful hair. In the end, Jim has a chain without a watch and Della a set of combs with little hair to be groomed. By sacrificing their most prized possessions, each gives the other the best Christmas gift of all. The story ends in their heartfelt, loving embrace.

This story is about intangibles. The two characters so love each other that each is willing to go to great lengths to make the other happy. Their gifts symbolize the bond they share, and what seems like foolishness is really a display of wisdom. At the end of the story, O. Henry remarks that the three wise men, the Magi, invented the practice of giving Christmas presents by bearing gifts to the child in the manger. He offers Della and Jim, the story's protagonists, the highest praise: "But in a last word to the wise of these days let it be said that of all who give gifts these two were the wisest. O all who give and receive gifts, such as they, are wisest. Everywhere they are wisest. They are the magi." The story implies we too can be such magi.

## The Journey of the Magi

Matthew's infancy narrative depicts the Magi as wise men who journeyed from the East to present the newborn king of the Jews gifts of gold, frankincense and myrrh. The star that guides them to the infant Jesus in the city of David, Bethlehem, represents their faith. According to tradition, these men, astrologers who searched the heavens for portents, followed this star because they believed it to be a sign from God.

Indeed, the star itself guided them to a distant place where God would reveal himself in a visible and tangible way. What they found at the end of their journey was not what they expected. Rather than a royal palace, they found a darkened cave. Rather than kingly trappings, they found a homeless family huddled against the cold, their infant lying in a manger, wrapped in swaddling clothes. God not only embraced the human condition, but did so in extreme poverty. With no room at the inn, only the warm breath of the stable animals kept the cold night air at bay.

God entered the world humbly, without airs. He came not with a clap of thunder, but in the silence of night. His angels proclaimed his coming not to kings in their courts, but to shepherds watching their sheep. Even the star that shone in Judea's western sky was modest and subdued, recognizable only to those who knew how to interpret the movements of the heavens. Many must have seen it, but failed to understand its significance. Many yearned for a sign, but did not know what to look for.

Only the wise men both saw the star and sensed its meaning. Only they had the faith and courage to follow wherever it led. Only they set out on a journey that would change their lives and that of every person who would ever live. Only they would greet God's gift to the world with gifts of their own: gold, frankincense, and myrrh. These gifts of Christmas, the first of their kind, signify Jesus' kingly status, his divine origins, and his impending death. Gold represents royalty; frankincense, the prayerful worship due to God alone; myrrh, the ointment that would embalm the body of the crucified Lord. Together, they point to the mystery of the Incarnation and the meaning of Jesus' name, "God saves." Centuries ago, the star of Bethlehem revealed God's saving power to a fallen world. Those who ponder the meaning of the star today, like the wise men of old, discover its light penetrating the dark, inner spaces of the human heart, where their newborn king has chosen to rest.

We live in a college town. One day we met a young man from Argentina, Juan, who had started coming to our parish. He actually joined a music ministry I was directing at the time. We soon discovered he was very talented and had a beautiful spirituality. Four years later, towards the end of his studies, he needed a place to stay until it was time for him to move to New York. My husband and I were happy to offer a space in our home and our children were thrilled to have him live with us. While he was with us, he spoke about a lay movement in which he grew up in back in Buenos Aires. While we found it interesting, we were a little afraid that it was something too "different" for us. We were very involved in our local church and concerned about getting into anything that would distract from that. Instead of trying to convince us, he simply invited us to attend a summer gathering in the Midwest region. Knowing Juan, we figured this could be a great experience for our family, so we decided to go. We even invited another family to join us. We can now see the great love of God for us through this invitation.

On our first day at this gathering, we saw the happiness that seemed to permeate everything and heard many, deeply impressive things.

We realized that we are part of a really big family, the family of God. All of a sudden, our world expanded, and our children were going off to take part in gatherings with other young people from all over the world! It was extraordinary. I began to see the divine in so many aspects of life. God was revealing his love to me in a very concrete way. When we try to live in the present moment and love well, it can change everything. We can really begin to build heaven on earth. The gospel helps me realize this and work toward doing my part. If I fail, as I often do, I know that I can begin again.

Each moment is a chance to love.[6]

## The Journey of Faith

We have much to learn from those wise men from the East who travelled great distances in search of the newborn king of the Jews. The gifts they gave pale in comparison to what they received. Their journey of faith and our own resemble each other.

To begin, the Magi represent the Gentile nations whence most Christians today come. We sometimes forget that most Christians have roots outside Jesus' own Jewish people. From the earliest days, through the efforts of the Apostle Peter (Acts 10: 1–48), the Apostle Paul (Acts 13:44–52), and a host of other zealous missionaries, Gentiles came to embrace the Gospel. Our faith is founded on the selfless efforts of these early disciples, in whose footsteps we are called to follow. The journey of the Magi reminds us that Christ's message is universal. All can become members of God's chosen people. The Magi also remind us that when darkness surrounds us, we too must travel by the dim light of faith.

The Magi, wise men studying the heavens for signs, found the star that led to Bethlehem. Their wisdom enabled them to decipher God's message hidden in the constellations of the night, but it was faith that inspired them to set out on their journey and eventually to lay their gifts at the feet of an infant lying in a manger. Where did such faith come from? The Magi themselves would never leave the comforts of their homelands for the hazards of a long journey in the desert, strangers in a foreign land, unless something outside themselves inspired them. What they hoped to gain from such a journey was not a typical object of desire—pleasure, power, possessions—but something intangible. They believed that this newborn king, whose star they saw rising (Mt 2:2) and whose coming the Scriptures predicted (Mt 2:5–6), would affect their lives and those of their people. For this reason they came to do him homage (Mt 2:11) and to lay their treasures before him (Mt 2:11–12). We are called to do likewise. Our faith journey leads to the feet of a newborn child whose mere presence in the world changes everything.

The journey of the Magi reveals that faith involves not merely intellectual assent but action based on our newfound beliefs. Once they discovered the signs in the night skies that pointed to the birth of a newborn king, they could have stayed home and let events simply take their course. Instead, they took upon themselves the hazards of a strenuous journey along the lonely, dark, and dangerous roads of ancient Palestine. Like the wise men, we too must not allow our faith to lie dormant, but put it into action. It is not enough simply to discern the signs of God's will for our lives. We must act on our conclusions and follow the path that the shining star of faith lights before us.

Their journey taught the Magi to expect the unexpected. They had no way to plan for every possible outcome. The discomforts and dangers of traveling by caravan included exposure to the elements, possible attack by highwaymen, even death at the hands of murderous rogues. Despite such hardships, they followed the star to Jerusalem and asked King Herod where they could find the newborn king of the Jews (Mt 2:1–2). He, in turn, learned from the chief priests and scribes that the Messiah would be born in Bethlehem of Judea (Mt 2:4–6). The wise men resumed their journey, eventually finding this newborn king not in a royal palace, but in a stable; dressed not in royal purple, but in swaddling clothes and lying in a manger. The journey of faith promises us similar unexpected risks and outcomes. The God of Abraham, Isaac and Jacob is also the God of surprises.

After leaving their gifts with the child and his parents, the Magi were warned in a dream not to go back to Herod, but to return to their own country by a different route. In effect, God instructed them to protect the newborn king of the Jews by not informing Herod of the infant's whereabouts, giving Joseph and Mary time to escape the king's murderous intentions by fleeing to Egypt. Their journey of faith made the Magi all the wiser, for through it they gained the capacity to read not only the external signs left by God in the heavens, but also the internal ones hidden in their dreams. We too become wiser when we search for the Christ child in the dark, interior reaches of our souls. By seeking him out in faith, we draw closer and are blessed with a deeper and more intimate knowledge of God's presence in our lives.

Finally, the Magi came to the Christ child bearing gifts, but from the outset of their journey to their return and beyond, God had blessed them with his own gift, the gift of faith. They were skilled in interpreting heavenly signs, but discernment of their meaning and the decision to follow them came not from themselves but from the divine power working within them. They were drawn to Christ by the power of the Holy Spirit at work in their hearts. Without some kind of incipient faith, they never would have set out pursuing the star in the first place. Nor would they have recognized in the tiny infant wrapped in swaddling clothes and lying in a manger the newborn king of the Jews. Their faith gave them eyes to see beneath appearances, to behold the deeper realities of life. Like the Magi, we too have been blessed with the gift of faith, which sheds light upon our path so that we can see past appearances to recognize Christ.

These are just a few of the insights we can learn from the Magi and their faithful journey to the Christ child. Although they came bearing precious gifts, they themselves received something far greater. It was faith that helped them see the significance of the star, and faith that sent them on their journey and led them to Bethlehem. This faith was not something of their own making, but a gift from God, the first of many he would shower upon the Gentile nations. We share in their legacy as we set out on our own journey of faith today, in search of Christ.

## Conclusion

Faith in Christ is a gift given by God and received with an open heart. It enables us to see more deeply into the mystery of life and to discover the meaning of existence. It helps us follow the true path down the highways and byways of life. It sheds light on that path, guiding us to our destination. Without faith life is aimless and incomplete. With faith life becomes a journey of discovery. It make us all magi in search of an infant child, "Emmanuel, God with us" (Mt 1:23–24), in the deepest recesses of our hearts.

Faith is freely bestowed upon all who seek God with sincere hearts. That is not to say, however, everyone who has received the gift of faith has explicit belief in Christ or even in God. Through no fault of their own, some people spend their lives searching for the truth and striving to lead good lives, but do not arrive at such beliefs during their lifetimes. The documents of the Second Vatican Council explain that goodness and truth, wherever found, are signs of God's gracious presence and a true preparation for the gospel (LG 16). What is not explicit in expressed beliefs is implicit in the way a person conducts his or her life. As with the Magi, God is busy preparing people's hearts long before they set out on their journey of faith and even longer before they fall down in homage and present their precious gifts to the newborn king.

Faith sends us on a journey to seek God's presence in every person, and in every time and circumstance. It gives our lives meaning and helps us extend that meaning to others. It deepens our trust in God and inspires us to befriend others. It enables us to see all that happens to us in the light of God's providential care. For a person of faith, everything has a purpose; everything has meaning; everything is gift. Faith is a most reasonable response to those who see life— indeed, existence itself—not as a problem to be solved but as a mystery to be revered.

## Reflection Questions

✦ Why is faith a gift? Why is it of God's making and not your own?

✦ How does human nature cause us to mistrust the actions and intentions of others? How does faith remedy that distrust?

✦ What lessons do you take from O. Henry's story, *The Gift of the Magi*?

✦ What have you learned from the story of the Magi in Matthew's Gospel?

✦ In what sense is faith in God a journey of discovery? In what sense is the journey itself a gift?

✦ Where is your star of Bethlehem? How did you discern its meaning? How has it led you to Christ?

## Living Faith

Lord, I thank you for the gift of faith. Let me never take it for granted. Let me never stray from its path. Help me to walk by its light. Let it accompany me in my journey. Let it penetrate the darkness before me and help me see the way I should walk. Deepen my faith in times of difficulty and hardship. By its power, help me at all times to trust in you and believe in you as you believe in me. Help me to treasure it and take it with me wherever I go. Lord, I believe in you. Help my unbelief. Help me to remain faithful to you at all times. Let me be forever grateful for this precious gift. *Mary, Mother of faith, pray for me.*

# 3

# Faith and Reason

Jews demand signs and Greeks desire wisdom,
but we proclaim Christ crucified, a stumbling-
block to Jews and foolishness to Gentiles, but
to those who are the called, both Jews and
Greeks, Christ the power of God and the
wisdom of God. For God's foolishness is wiser
than human wisdom, and God's weakness is
stronger than human strength.

*1 Cor 1:22–25*

S ome individuals find no foundation in reason for
faith. Because they perceive no basis for it in sound
human judgment, they consider it irrational. People
of faith, such skeptics say, live in an imaginary
world. A truly rational person would affirm that God
does not exist or, at the very least, cannot be known with
certitude. Since God's existence cannot be demonstrated or
verified empirically, they consider "the God question" to
be irrelevant. Morality and sound ethical behavior, these
skeptics point out, do not flow from religious convictions
alone and can easily be separated from their presumed basis
in faith. They also note how throughout history religion has
repeatedly generated war, and still today inspires much of
the violence in the world. They agree with John Lennon's
song, *Imagine*, that the world would be better without a
heaven and with no religion.

Many hold with this negative view towards faith, as does
secular society, which has tried to marginalize the impact of
faith in public life.

At one point in my life, I found such arguments persuasive, and did not know how to respond to them. As I matured in my faith, however, I came to see the fundamental flaws in such opinions, which rest upon false or only partially true assumptions. When scrutinized, their foundations waver and they collapse like a house of cards.

## The Case against Faith

Those who hold solely with reason assert that faith is not a valid way of knowing because its claims are unverifiable. Throughout history, they argue, many religions have arisen out of human imagination, not human reason. God is merely a mental construct. He did not create human beings; we created him. We did so because of the unbearable horror at the thought of being alone in the universe, abandoned in an existential abyss of nothingness. God is only a projection of our deepest needs and desires.

Thus, believing in God is mere wish fulfillment, a self-made fantasy. Believers have deluded themselves that there is something beyond this life, even though they have no concrete evidence for it. Their convenient, self-perpetuating belief system can be verified only after death. Such people are wasting their lives on a dream that will never come true, letting real life pass them by as they hope for an afterlife. People of faith rely on God because they are afraid to rely on themselves. The one they are waiting for never came and will never return; God never existed.

Skeptics observe that faith has done the world more harm than good. They observe that religion has generated endless controversy, inciting people not only to die for their faith, but also to kill for it. The Bible is full of examples of men and women pursuing their own desires, often violently, in the name of God. Throughout history, faith has been invoked to wage wars, torture individuals, burn the innocent, and starve the poor and helpless. Threatened by

*Christopher Hitchens, the talented writer who called himself an "antitheist," reflected on his own impending death after he had received a diagnosis of esophageal cancer. In this excerpt from his* Vanity Fair *essay, "Topic of Cancer," he demonstrates with characteristic honesty and clarity the meaning of life for someone who cannot profess faith in God.*

In one way, I suppose, I have been "in denial" for some time, knowingly burning the candle at both ends and finding that it often gives a lovely light. But for precisely that reason, I can't see myself smiting my brow with shock or hear myself whining about how it's all so unfair: I have been taunting the Reaper into taking a free scythe in my direction and have now succumbed to something so predictable and banal that it bores even me. Rage would be beside the point for the same reason. Instead, I am badly oppressed by a gnawing sense of waste. I had real plans for my next decade and felt I'd worked hard enough to earn it. Will I really not live to see my children married? To watch the World Trade Center rise again? …. But I understand this sort of non-thinking for what it is: sentimentality and self-pity. Of course my book hit the best-seller list on the day that I received the grimmest of news bulletins, and for that matter the last flight I took as a healthy-feeling person (to a fine, big audience at the Chicago Book Fair) was the one that made me a million-miler on United Airlines, with a lifetime of free upgrades to look forward to. But irony is my business and I just can't see any ironies here: would it be less poignant to get cancer on the day that my memoirs were remaindered as a box-office turkey, or that I was bounced from a coach-class flight and left on the tarmac? To the dumb question "Why me?" the cosmos barely bothers to return the reply: Why not? [7]

the progress of science, believers have gone to great lengths to impede its growth. Because faith confuses fantasy with reality, it is dangerous.

## The Case against Reason

There is, of course, another side to the argument. Claims against faith in the name of reason overlook the ways in which reason itself has been redefined. What was considered "reasonable" in one epoch became "out of date" or even obsolete in another.

Take biblical interpretation, for example. During the patristic period, fathers of the Church commonly based their interpretation of allegorical passages on patterns in the Bible. For example, the Exodus story of the Jews was typically seen as a reflection of humanity's journey from the slavery of sin to the fullness of life in Christ. This approach reflected the dominant philosophy of that era, Neo-Platonism, which asserted that patterns of thought shared in an otherworldly realm of pre-existent Ideas. During the Scholastic period of the high Middle Ages, allegory gave way to syllogistic reasoning. Using Aristotelian logic, scholars no longer searched for hidden patterns, but for rational arguments. Medieval synthesis was supplanted by Nominalism, a method of analysis more focused on particulars, associated with development of the scientific method and its insistence upon empirical verification. Among biblical scholars, this method manifested itself in a concern for historical context, literary form, authorial intent, and redaction history. Like any other literary text, the Bible was carefully scrutinized for what it revealed about the author, the audience, and the author's reasons for writing. The movement in biblical interpretation from allegory to syllogistic reasoning to critical historical analysis shows how the criteria of reason have changed over time.

Indeed, throughout the history of Western thought reason has been reinvented to correspond with an ever-narrower understanding of its limits and criteria for its affirmations of truth. By the latter half of the nineteenth century, reason had nothing else on which to turn its razor-sharp edge but itself; doing so led to its own demise. The notion of reason itself thus became the very instrument by which the masters of suspicion (Marx, Freud and Nietzsche) forced open the cracks in the foundation of reason's fortress, allowing its seemingly impregnable walls to collapse. This event in intellectual history marked the end of the modern era and the beginning of what became known as postmodernism.

This systematic dismantling of reason's rule over the last 150 years was achieved by working from the inside out. Deconstructionism, the systematic disassembling of rational discourse, was a logical outgrowth of the Enlightenment's fascination with the power of human reason. Amidst the debris of discontinuities and broken concepts deconstructionism has left behind, a unique opportunity arose in the history of Western thought and culture: the retrieval of recently discounted elements of its rich philosophical and theological tradition and the possible reintegration of its moral and spiritual horizons.

## Faith and Reason

Reason's self-analysis has brought into question its very foundations. Some contemporary philosophers recognize that, in fact, several rationalities are at work in the world, each embedded in a particular tradition with its own set of operating assumptions and principles.[8]

In the Catholic tradition, reason has an encompassing scope. It upholds the essential unity of truth which it identifies with the Logos, the Eternal Word of God. In this tradition every rationality participates to some extent in Wisdom, although some more than others. The Catholic tradition refuses to narrow the scope of reason by limiting truth only to what can be empirically verified. It recognizes the value of allegory, syllogistic reasoning and the scientific method, using each approach when appropriate. Because truth is one, it also rejects the theories developed by Boethius of Dacia and Siger of Brabant in the thirteenth century, which acknowledge a "double truth"—a truth of faith and a parallel (even contradictory) truth of reason.[9] Nor does it relinquish the reasonableness of faith as did the nineteenth-century Danish philosopher Søren Kierkegaard, who considered faith a leap into and an embrace of the absurd.[10] In the Catholic tradition, faith is preeminently reasonable. It recognizes the limitations of human reason and its inability to exhaust the truth. It also has the humility to acknowledge humanity's dependence upon a power beyond itself. In the words of Augustine, "You have made us for yourself, and our hearts are restless until they can find peace in you."[11]

The most comprehensive Catholic treatment of the relationship between faith and reason is John Paul II's encyclical, *Fides et Ratio* (1998). This letter posits an organic unity between faith and reason, and claims the two can work in harmony. Without reason, faith can lose its footing in the real world and lead to superstition; without faith, however, reason can devolve into relativism and agnosticism. Right reason (*ratio recta*) can perceive and then formulate the first universal principles of being. From these principles, coherent logical and ethical conclusions follow (FR 4).

The Church does not "canonize any one particular philosophy in preference to others" (FR 49), and the pope laments the "philosophical pride" of some scholars who consider their partial and limited perspective a total presentation of the truth (FR 4). He also points out that modern philosophy in particular has taken some wrong turns that have led to error (FR 49). For this reason, the Church must scrutinize those philosophical positions that contradict Christian doctrine. Its teaching office has the obligation not only to point out such positions, but also to articulate what faith requires of philosophy (FR 50).

## Faith Seeking Understanding

The classical definition of theology as *fides quaerens intellectum* ("faith seeking understanding") conveys the distinctive yet harmonious functions of faith and reason in the pursuit of meaning.[12] Certain consequences flow from this mutual relationship.

Faith and reason relate to each other only if they maintain their distinct identities. Neither is served when one imposes itself upon the other's domain. Subsuming faith into reason—or vice versa—does a disservice to each and endangers their individual and mutual possibilities. Christianity, for example, maintains that the God who created and who sustains the universe revealed himself in the person of Jesus Christ. This fundamental premise is the reasonable and credible starting point from which flow the remaining articles of Christian faith. Because proving or disproving this fundamental premise lies beyond the scope of human reason, all attempts to do so are ultimately ideological. Similarly, faith opens itself to rightful criticism when it is used as the basis for argument in areas beyond its competence, as in the infamous "Scopes Monkey Trial" of 1925 when William Jennings Bryan cited biblical passages to support scientific phenomena, thus opening scripture to Clarence Darrow's mockery.

Faith proceeds from following Christ and adhering to the truths of revelation as interpreted by the Church's teaching office. Faith engages the whole person, intellectually and ethically. Belief in Christ requires not only intellectual assent, but also the determination to live as one of his disciples. Its distinctive nature is both private and communal. God imparts the gift of faith to an individual through the community. Never completely private, its fundamental purpose is participation in Christ's body, the Church. The distinctiveness of faith also flows from its divine origin; it cannot exist without grace. Belief in Christ is not a merely human action. Only under the influence of grace can a person make a free and wholehearted decision to follow him.

Reason corresponds with human nature. Although at times it operates intuitively, its primary focus is to process words, images, and ideas discursively. Unlike angels, who think entirely on the intuitive level, or animals, who act according to their instincts, human beings think discursively. Human reason is a single process, but has speculative and practical dimensions. As such, it possesses a fundamental openness to reality and can make sound judgments based on common sense. The scope of right reason includes pure logic, but goes far beyond it. Because of its openness to reality, informed by faith and elevated by the gifts of the Holy Spirit, it can be receptive to God's grace. In particular, the Spirit's gifts of wisdom, understanding, counsel, and knowledge endow human beings with the ability to know God intimately, understand the truths of faith, give prudent advice, and make proper judgments about the things of this world. Because of humanity's fall from grace, human reason is limited and flawed. It is healed, made whole, and even elevated through the movement of grace, the influence of faith, and the work of the Spirit.

Through right reason faith acquires a wealth of benefits. For one thing, the truths of revelation can be examined in an organized and systematic manner. The great textbooks of theology from the Scholastic era (*Summae*) demonstrate reason's capacity to penetrate the truths of revelation, analyze them in a respectful and coherent manner, collate them according to themes, and synthesize them into a cohesive whole. Popular catechisms demonstrate reason's capacity to simplify the truths of faith for a wide audience. Preachers and homilists use reason to convince the minds and convert the hearts of their listeners. In modern times, reason serves faith by promoting the Christian message through newspapers, radio, television, movies, the internet and other social media. Reason enables Christians to examine, probe, question, develop and communicate the truths of revelation on many levels, making us all the richer for it.

Faith also broadens reason and deepens it. Because of humanity's fall from grace, reason has faltered and diminished. Ignorance and pride limit its full potential. They infect the human capacity to know both by clouding and by overinflating reason. As a human faculty, making reason an object of worship is a mistake. Separated from their source in Divine Wisdom, rational powers—either reason or will (the rational appetite)—overstep their bounds, as happened in Adam's and Eve's attempt to be like gods (Gn 3:1–7). Through faith, the limited nature and weakened state of reason is acknowledged, purging it of hubris. Reason is opened up to a capacious vision of reality that places at the center of the universe not self, but God. Its wounds healed, human reason achieves an unprecedented status. Informed by faith and strengthened by grace, reason acquires the capacity to see beyond earthly horizons and so enter into a profound experience of the gospel.

Faith and reason complement each other. They do not operate in parallel or mutually exclusive worlds. There is no truth of faith or truth of reason—truth is one. Understood truly, they cannot be ignorant of or opposed to one other. Apparent inconsistencies and contradictions betray the limited power of human comprehension. No human being can understand the mind of God. As the Lord said to the prophet Isaiah, "My thoughts are not your thoughts, nor are your ways my ways" (Is 55:8). Nevertheless, without faith reason cannot probe and understand the meaning of revealed truths. And with faith, reason is prevented from overextending itself into pride. Together, faith and reason complement each other for the good of individuals and society as a whole. Set against each other, they tear one

another down, pit individuals one against the other, and
break down society's religious institutions.

Like two lungs that work together for the good of
the same organism, faith and reason must maintain their
distinct identities yet work in harmony. The Second Vatican
Council affirms: "God, the beginning and end of all things,
can be known with certainty from created reality by the
light of human reason; but...it is through His revelation that
those religious truths which are by their nature accessible to
human reason can be known by all men with ease, with solid
certitude and with no trace of error, even in this present
state of the human race" (DV 6).

## Conclusion

The Catholic philosopher Blaise Pascal (1623–62)
acknowledged that even if rational thought cannot prove
God's existence, belief offers more advantages than
unbelief. Therefore, it would be reasonable to wager on
God's existence and to live accordingly. At the end of life,
if it turned out that God does exist, the wager would yield
an eternal reward for a life well lived. If God does not, then
the bettor would still have the benefit of having lived a good
and virtuous life.[13]

An expert mathematician, Pascal makes a convincing
case for faith based on the probability of outcomes and an
understanding of rationality's limits. His wager demonstrates
how belief in God, even under the constraints of the strictest
logic, can be considered reasonable. Pascal recognizes that
life involves knowing how to live with uncertainty; belief in
God is no exception. His hypothetical wager demonstrates
the underlying rationality of faith and describes a situation
in which faith and reason stay focused on the same distant
horizon, albeit from different perspectives.

This chapter has presented the benefits of faith and
reason working in harmony for a common purpose. Without

compromising their distinctive identities, they can work together in the service of truth. Faith and reason provide a mutual benefit; each has something to give and receive from the other. This relationship outlines a theological concept that, properly understood, lies at the very heart of Christian spirituality—"faith seeking understanding."

## Reflection Questions

✧ What are the distinctive characteristics of faith?

✧ What are the distinctive characteristics of reason?

✧ How do you understand the relationship between faith and reason? Does one oppose the other? Is one superior to the other? Are they both valid ways of knowing?

✧ What has been your view of the relationship between faith and reason? Has it changed over time? Which of the two is more important to you?

✧ What is their relationship of faith and reason to truth? Do they lead to the same or separate truths? How can you tell the difference?

✧ When do faith and reason work together in the service of truth? When do they work against it?

✧ Can you point to concrete experiences in your own life of how faith and reason worked together?

## Living Faith

Lord, I thank you for the gift of faith and for the capacity to probe its mysteries with my mind. I am grateful for the rational grounding of my faith and for the way faith completes reason and makes it whole. Let me never take either of them for granted. Help me to recognize their distinctive traits, the boundaries between them, and the common ground they share. Teach me how they work together in service of the truth. Show me how they can do so in my own life so that I might have a deeper awareness of your presence in my life. *Mary, Mother of faith, pray for me.*

# 4

# Faith and Prayer

Ask, and it will be given to you; search, and you will find; knock, and the door will be opened for you. For everyone who asks receives, and everyone who searches finds, and for everyone who knocks, the door will be opened. Is there anyone among you who, if your child asks for bread, will give a stone? Or if the child asks for a fish, will give a snake? If you then, who are evil, know how to give good gifts to your children, how much more will your Father in heaven give good things to those who ask him!

*Mt 7:7–11*

During my twenty years in Rome as a professor of theology, I once met a person who, despite being an avowed atheist, regularly attended the sung Latin High Mass for its rich cultural value. He went to Mass not to pray, but to appreciate its aesthetic beauty in much the same way a person would go to a museum, attend a concert, or admire a work of art. Although I commended him for going to church, I could not help but feel he was overlooking something important. The Mass, after all, is not a work of art or a cultural artifact, but the living prayer of the Church. To go to Mass and not pray is like going to a movie with dark glasses and plugs in one's ears. To do so is to pass up a much deeper experience.

Perhaps you are a devout Catholic who would never go to Mass only as a spectator. Perhaps you are not Catholic, and attend other religious services. If you find that this story doesn't apply to your life, ask yourself the following questions. Do I go to church to give or to take? Do I attend worship because of what I get out of it, or to render glory and praise to God? Do I go there on Sunday mornings because it makes me feel good, perhaps even better than other people, or to express my gratitude and love to God? When attending Mass Catholics would do well to keep in mind the words of St. Alphonsus de Liguori (1696–1787): "One single Mass gives more honor to God than all the penances of the saints, the labors of the Apostles, the sufferings of the martyrs, and even the burning love of the Blessed Mother of God." Our primary motive for attending church services should be to worship God. All else is secondary.

My encounter with this "devout" Italian atheist brought to mind the close relationship between faith and prayer. Without faith prayer is false and inauthentic; without prayer faith withers and dies. Prayer is an act of faith; faith, in turn, is a basic requirement for prayer. Prayer deepens faith; faith makes prayer possible. Together, they foster intimacy with God. Separate them, and each becomes an empty shell. Like a tree whose roots seek life-giving water, faith seeks out prayer and depends on it to survive and grow.

## Intellectual Faith

Some individuals do believe in God yet never pray. For example, someone with a strictly intellectual approach, who considers faith solely in terms of affirming the body of truths in a creed or a catechism, may not perceive a need for prayer. It is possible, in other words, for a person to have faith but, for whatever reason, not seek God's help in any way. Some people do seem to live totally inside their heads. Such individuals might know a great deal about faith and even assent to it intellectually, but make little or no attempt to converse with God. At times, even committed believers can "live in their heads" by over rationalizing their beliefs and not allowing them to take flesh in actions. Separating mind from heart, thought from feelings, can lead to fragmented, inauthentic lives that diminish the witness value of faith.

Such an incomplete, merely intellectual understanding of faith can be fleshed out through approaches that fulfill a person's physical, emotional, spiritual, and social needs. If it is authentic, faith engages not one single aspect of human existence or another, but the whole person. By itself, any one approach to faith needs to be complemented by others. An intellectual approach emphasizes the content of faith and the truths of revelation. Its weakness, however, lies in the tendency to overlook other elements of human makeup that cry out for more personal contact with God. The intellect, then, finds completeness in other aspects of Christian spirituality such as love, friendship, service to others and, of course, prayer.

Moreover, to be true to itself even a strictly intellectual approach acknowledges that "Catholic faith"—that is, the very truth of Christianity itself—requires believers to engage God in private prayer and to worship in community. To do otherwise would contradict some of the very truths Christians profess. Faith requires believers to worship God with open minds and hearts. The intellectual side of life should remain connected with the other dimensions of human makeup. An authentic faith, of whatever kind, must never cease seeking God in prayer. A person of faith must strive to be a person of prayer—and vice versa.

## Faith as Trust

Understanding faith as trust complements intellectual faith and highlights how prayer sustains the relationship between God and God's people. Here, faith means trusting God in good times as well as bad, regardless of the surrounding people or circumstances. The prophet Jeremiah highlights the importance of this element of trust

# Faith and Prayer

Some years ago, Mary and I figured out our taxes as we usually did at the end of February. We always did them as early as possible so that our tax refunds, which were substantial because of our large family, would come back sooner. This time, however, we were shocked to discover that we owed the government $900.... At that time we lived literally from paycheck to paycheck and had no savings. We were really getting worried because we didn't know what to do.

We decided to go to the Newman Center chapel nearby. Since the chapel was empty we sat down in front of the tabernacle and said: "You are God, so you know what we need. You gave us many children and we always trusted that you would help us take care of them. They are your children more than ours. We need your help now. Next month, on April 15, we need exactly $900." Right away we felt peaceful. We got up and went back home.

The following week the dean at my school asked if I could go to Bridgeport, Connecticut, to speak about our school's program for faculty and curricular development.... The stipend would be $250. What immediately crossed my mind was, "This is God's first installment on the tax bill."

Then Mary was asked to present a workshop on homeopathy and first-aid for parents. She prepared a whole-day program for parents, who came from near and far upon recommendations from their doctors. This installment amounted to another $200.

I was asked to give another talk and was paid $150, and then we got another $50 unexpectedly. Three days before April 15 we had a total of $600. Even though we still needed $300, God was doing such a great job with his surprises up to that point that we were confident he would not stop.

We prayed that night and the next day, and sometimes started to doubt and worry, but we kept on praying. On April 14, in our mail was an envelope with the return address of an old friend who had not written in years: "Dear Tom, I'm doing well, but I feel that you and Mary may need some help right now. Love to you both, Pat."

Inside was his check for $300.[14]

with a striking image of life amid the desert: "Blessed are those who trust in the Lord, whose trust is the Lord. They shall be like a tree planted by water, sending out its roots by the stream. It shall not fear when heat comes, and its leaves shall stay green; in the year of drought it is not anxious, and it does not cease to bear fruit" (Jer 17:7–8).

Those who trust in God are like a tree that sends its roots out in search of life-giving water. In such a setting those rooted in God and trusting in his benevolent care need not fear present or future hardships. God cares, loves his people and wants what is best for them. What is more, he trusts them more than they trust themselves. Why else would he endow human beings with the ability to distinguish right from wrong and the freedom to become his close, intimate friends?

Although God may trust his people, they often fail to reciprocate. All too often, they prefer to rely on themselves than seek him in prayer. They think that they can manage the worries and concerns of daily life but can easily be thrown off balance, leaving them lost, without purpose or direction. Human beings find it difficult to trust God on their own. They cannot do it by themselves. Through prayer, however, they can remain rooted in God. Through prayer, they search out the waters of divine love and do not rest until they find it. The Second Vatican Council's *Constitution on the Sacred Liturgy* states: "The spiritual life ... is not limited solely to participation in the liturgy. The Christian is indeed called to pray with his brethren, but he must also enter into his chamber to pray to the Father, in secret; yet more, according to the teaching of the Apostle, he should 'pray without ceasing' " (1 Thes 5:17; SC 12).

Over the centuries, Christians have implemented many interpretations of what it means to "pray without ceasing." Some start each day by offering the actions of their day in a single prayer. Others, like those who recite the Divine Office, make the day holy by stopping at regular intervals of the day to recite the Psalms. Yet others say the "Jesus

Prayer," that is, reciting the Holy Name of Jesus over and over until, resonating deeply in their hearts, it forms a continuous backdrop for their awareness. Some allow the deepest yearning of their hearts to rise to the surface of their awareness. Still others simply live in communion with God. Whatever the interpretation, all are called to make prayer more and more an integral, important part of daily life.

## The Ways of Prayer

Prayer means entering into relationship with, conversing with, and remaining in communion with God. The many forms of this "great means of salvation" relate to faith in many ways.

Prayer both requires faith and expresses it. It makes no sense to attempt a conversation with someone who does not exist. Those who pray do so because they believe God exists and listens to them. Prayer is a conversation, a dialogue. Speaking to God in prayer affirms belief in his personal nature and his interest in our well-being. Those who pray do so not to appease God or satisfy an obligation, but to deepen a relationship with him. Speaking to God means telling him what is on our minds and in our hearts. God, in turn, speaks to those who pray through the people they meet, in the events of the day, in the silence of their hearts, and in their meditative reading of the Scriptures. Prayer presupposes and reinforces belief. Without faith, prayer cannot happen. At the same time, prayer deepens and completes faith.

There are various forms of prayer—*oratio* (vocal prayer), *meditatio* (meditation), *contemplatio* (contemplation)—to accompany the journey in faith. Children just developing speech learn to pray vocally. As their minds develop and thoughts filled with images and concepts begin to form, they discover how to meditate. The richness of silence as a means of intimate communication allows contemplation. These various forms of prayer offer assurance that anyone can turn his or her mind and heart to God at any moment in the faith journey. They are reminders that, as they do with any other person, individuals can relate to God in a variety of ways. As faith matures, prayer deepens, bringing intimacy with God.

Faith seeks to permeate human life and penetrate every level of being: the physical, emotional, intellectual, spiritual and social. Prayer enables faith to do that. Prayer uses the body, words, gestures, fasting, hymns, art—every human means of communication. Meditation opens the mind and heart to God. At moments of rest in silence or before the Blessed Sacrament, our spirits rise to God in contemplation. Attending Mass, reciting the breviary, or joining in a prayer meeting lets individuals stand with the believing community. Authentic prayer brings faith with it wherever it goes. It seeks to incorporate all aspects of human makeup into a relationship with God. Prayer is the way faith touches every dimension of human existence to make it fully alive for God.

Prayer and faith depend on each other. Although without faith prayer does not exist, without prayer faith cannot flourish. Prayer deepens faith by helping believers know God personally. The more that minds and hearts are open to God, the more individuals learn to trust him in all things. Prayer leads from knowing about God to a living, intimate friendship with him. The deeper the friendship with God, the more profound faith becomes. While faith enables us to approach God in prayer, prayer deepens faith in God and enables us to trust God in all things and at all times. Prayer, like faith, is a divine gift. No one can pray without God's help, yet he offers this grace to everyone. Through prayer God calls us to himself and offers us his friendship. It enables the human person to relate to God as one close, intimate friend to another.

Both faith and prayer are oriented toward life in the Spirit. Prayer, be it ascetical or mystical, requires God's grace. In ascetical prayer the individual remains the primary actor; in mystical prayer the Holy Spirit gradually takes over. This important distinction is also reflected in the life of faith. As faith matures, believers live the gospel with ever deeper levels of awareness. In time, the individual's role in the act of faith decreases and that of the Spirit increases. As St. Paul tells the Galatians, "It is no longer I who live, but it is Christ who lives in me" (Gal 2:20). Through the influence of the Spirit, knowledge of God becomes more experiential, leading to a meeting face-to-face. This encounter deepens trust in God's care and develops a sense of security. As Paul himself reminds the Church at Rome, "If God is for us, who is against us?" (Rom 8:31).

Finally, faith and prayer are ultimately transformed by participation in the resurrection of Christ and life in the world beyond. The resurrection involves a radical transformation of our entire being. While this changed existence will be continuous with what went before it, it will also elevate us to a higher state. Faith and prayer themselves will be transformed. As the Spirit takes on a greater role in a person's life, doubts fade, uncertainty turns into certainty, faith becomes vision and comprehension. Through deep intimacy with God, believers will never risk losing their faith or falling out of communion with God or with the other members of Christ's body, the Church. Faith and prayer will no longer depend on each other because they will converge into a single, life-giving, eternal hymn of praise.

These few insights suggest how faith and prayer influence each other, maintain their distinctive identities, and draw closer in the life of the Spirit. While these observations in no way exhaust the possibilities of this relationship, they highlight the main contours of their ongoing interaction and point to a way they ultimately converge in the face-to-face encounter with God in the life beyond.

## Conclusion

So close is the relationship between faith and prayer that it often goes unnoticed. Faith is the backdrop against which prayer operates on behalf of the individual and the believing community. Without it, prayer would be only the empty expression of false, inauthentic selves. Prayer, in turn, gives faith a voice, one that resonates within human hearts and is heard by God. Without it, faith loses its heart and inner vibrancy.

Prayer and faith are like two sides of a coin. One cannot truly be itself without the other. Separating them would disfigure them and ultimately disrupt life. For this reason, individuals must appropriate the ways of prayer with care so that they parallel their process of maturation in faith. Teaching individuals the faith without imparting the ways of prayer deprives them of the living relationship with God so vital to spiritual life. Teaching the ways of prayer without conveying a sound understanding of the faith can make them stray from the path of truth and holiness.

The close relationship between faith and prayer demonstrates the essential role of each in becoming more fully alive for God. Together, they accompany us through life, help us become ourselves in the faith, and bring us to safe haven.

## Reflection Questions

✦ How do faith and prayer interact in your own life? Have they ever existed apart from one another?

✦ Have you ever found yourself believing in God but not praying because you do not want to bother him, or because he would not be interested in your petty problems?

✧ Have you ever found yourself praying but wondering whether God hears you?

✧ Have you ever found yourself praying and wondering whether God even exists?

✧ Why is prayer so important for faith?

✧ Why is faith so important for prayer?

✧ How do faith and prayer complement each other? What can they learn from each other?

✧ Has your prayer life kept pace with your growth in faith?

✧ How does your faith shape the way you relate to God?

## Living Faith

Lord, teach me to pray. Show me the different ways of prayer and help me to use them for your greater glory. Through them, deepen my faith so I may come to seek you at all times and in all circumstances. Let my prayer penetrate my faith, and my faith my prayer. Let them both penetrate every aspect of my being so without ceasing I may lift my mind and heart to you. Help me to be a true disciple: a person of deep faith and authentic prayer. Help me to seek you at all times and to trust you without counting the cost. *Mary, Mother of faith, pray for me.*

# 5

# Faith and Suffering

> We are afflicted in every way, but not
> crushed; perplexed, but not driven to despair;
> persecuted, but not forsaken; struck down, but
> not destroyed; always carrying in the body the
> death of Jesus, so that the life of Jesus may
> also be made visible in our bodies. For while
> we live, we are always being given up to death
> for Jesus' sake, so that the life of Jesus may be
> made visible in our mortal flesh. So death is at
> work in us, but life in you.
>
> *2 Cor 4:8–12*

In May of 2010, after a diagnosis of ALL (Acute Lymphocytic Leukemia), I went through a long, harrowing treatment. In the space of a year and a half, I spent close to eight months in the hospital, receiving intense chemotherapy treatments at three different medical centers. After a relapse I participated in two separate clinical trials to get back into remission and finally received a bone marrow transplant at Memorial Sloan-Kettering Cancer Center in New York. My recovery from this deadly disease progresses, but I face a future of continued health monitoring and the possibility of yet another relapse.

I cite this experience not to draw attention to myself but to make a simple point: suffering is a part of life that often comes when least expected. Before my diagnosis I was healthy and physically fit, looking forward to many more years of life. I did not think I would have to worry about a life-threatening illness for many years to come—if at all. Cancer was the furthest thing from my mind.

All that changed. The leukemia came out of nowhere, took away much of my independence and left me unable to care for myself in some of the most basic ways. The disease took its toll not only on my body, but also on my psychological and spiritual well-being. When I look back on all that happened—physical decline, sadness, self-pity, loss of control, uncertainty about my future, anger, the confrontation with death—one question stands out: Where would I be without faith?

## Suffering without Faith

I sometimes try to imagine what it would be like to face a life-threatening illness without the support of faith. I respect any person's choice to accept the gift of faith or to reject it. At the same time, I have difficulty understanding how someone with a potentially fatal illness could face the harsh realities of impending death without faith. Such a person has no prospects beyond the grave. Disease becomes an unfortunate fact of life; suffering has no meaning; life simply ends with death. With no hope for life after death, he or she may seek to live on through children or by making a mark on history.

These attempts at vicarious immortality, however, fade with the passage of years. Most people are forgotten within a few generations. With the endless march of time, a person's legacy grows faint. Few are fortunate enough to have an impact that spans the ages. Against the backdrop of the age of the universe, moreover, any person's trace, however notable, dwindles to insignificance.

Except for considering one's children or one's accomplishments as a way of living on after death, a person without faith in God and a belief in the afterlife has few options but to be resigned to the hardships and limitations of life. From such a perspective, suffering and death are a natural part of life. We are born. We live. We suffer. We die. We try to

# Suffering and Faith

"I was close to finishing my first year as a fourth-grade teacher. This was the fun part of the year filled with award ceremonies and field trips, but God had other plans." Beth-Anne's limbs had started to fall asleep easily, followed by episodes of dizziness and vertigo. Then one morning she felt pressure in the back of her head, followed by a tingling sensation in her legs. By evening, she headed to the emergency room. "On the way to the ER," Beth-Anne says, "I sent a text message asking my friends for their prayers. Immediately, my cell phone was buzzing with supportive responses. I felt at peace; I was not alone. I was living this with them and for them."

"While in the hospital I was amazed at the love and support of friends…. Clare, in the middle of studying for finals and preparing for a presentation, came just to be with me in the hospital. When she had to leave, Paul who was also in the middle of studying for finals, came and waited for two hours while I was getting MRIs done…."

"The more I worked, the worse my symptoms became. I had to take medical leave. I began to understand more that the only thing that matters is to love. This I could do, love. And I could use these moments to gain an appreciation of those who also suffer. I reflected on my younger brother who had been ill and out of school for a long time. Until this experience, I did not know how to show him the compassion he deserved because I did not grasp his suffering. I began to feel closer to him. This insight alone was worth the whole experience…."

"I realize that I might never discover what has caused this sickness, or be healed of it. But I have been able to let go of some thoughts and habits that kept me away from God. This all is happening out of God's love for me. When I think of how much I've gained from this experience, I feel like I haven't lost anything."[15]

avoid suffering as much as possible and ameliorate its effects when it comes, but somewhere in our future we know it awaits us. In the face of such a future, we measure our worth by our contributions to society, by the power or pleasure we have managed to squeeze out of life, or by not measuring it at all. Since death comes to everyone—good or evil, rich or poor, happy or sad—many consider suffering and the end of life as the final whimper of a meaningless existence. Despair becomes their only alternative and they feel angry, raging at their impending doom. For these, suffering points to nothing beyond itself but death and non-existence.

## Faith and Suffering

With Christian faith, those who suffer find meaning in their experience. They are able to understand that the suffering they have undergone and will undergo is a sharing in the passion and death of Jesus Christ. The explanation seems almost too good to be true. God was and is so madly in love with human beings that he chose to enter our world as one of us, give himself to us completely, nourish us with his body and blood, and become for us a life-giving source of hope. Through Jesus' life, death and resurrection, suffering and death no longer have a hold over us. Jesus has set us free to love and to become ourselves.

Jesus' suffering transforms our own life and gives it new meaning. With the power of love he overcame death, giving us hope that one day we too might rise with him. Faith in Jesus enables us to look beyond suffering and death. It deepens trust in the power of love and the hope of sharing in his transformed existence. The Second Vatican Council affirms: "On earth, still as pilgrims in a strange land, tracing in trial and in oppression the paths He trod, we are made one with His sufferings like the body is one with the Head, suffering with Him, that with Him we may be glorified" (LG 7). Faith brings about this change in outlook by giving suffering purpose and direction. It does so by allowing us to enter into and share in the narrative of Jesus' passion, death and resurrection. God loved us so much that he gave us a role to play in the world's redemption. He has allowed the members of his body, the Church, to participate in Christ's paschal mystery. With faith, suffering can be salvific like Christ's.

Christ's Church includes members who participate in varying degrees: "All men are called to be part of this catholic unity of the people of God which in promoting universal peace presages it. And there belong to or are related to it in various ways, the Catholic faithful, all who believe in Christ and indeed the whole of mankind, for all men are called by the grace of God to salvation" (LG 13). Depending on a person's upbringing, cultural background and education, faith in Christ can be explicit or implicit. The more a person is aware of Christ's presence in his or her life, the greater his or her understanding of the connection between human suffering and Christ's. Such awareness and understanding permit the free and open acceptance of suffering as a part of God's plan for each person's life, the unhesitating embrace of the cross of Christian discipleship. That is precisely what happened to me as I struggled to come to terms with my leukemia. I slowly came to view my suffering as intimately bound up with the suffering of Christ. What is more, St. Paul's words resonated deep within my heart: "We are afflicted in every way, but not crushed; perplexed, but not driven to despair; persecuted, but not forsaken; struck down, but not destroyed; always carrying in the body the death of Jesus, so that the life of Jesus may also be made visible in our bodies" (2 Cor 4:8–10).

## Embracing the Cross

Those who have faith in Christ can take up their cross daily and walk the path of discipleship. Through faith they trust God in all things—trials, disease, even persecution. Such discipleship has a cost—carrying one's cross.

God rarely allows individuals to choose their own cross. All too often, crosses appear suddenly, unexpectedly: the loss of a job, foreclosure on a house, the unexpected death of child, the sudden onslaught of a debilitating or life-threatening disease. Such unexpected burdens cause suffering on many levels: physical, emotional, intellectual, spiritual, even social. Sometimes these crosses remain for extended periods, leaving no way to avoid or escape them: a crippling war injury, an addiction, long-term unemployment. We may dream about being spared one particular cross and choosing another, but life does not work like that. What makes life *our* story—uniquely ours in all the world—is its highly personal, intense and unpredictable nature. The crosses that appear are the ones we are being asked to carry. Our task is to bear whatever trials come our way with courage and dignity.

Bearing trials and suffering in this fashion does not mean escaping the pain or pretending suffering does not exist. Suffering is not an illusion. It cannot be ignored or wished away. It is real. It must be confronted. Jesus looked suffering and death in the eye and asks us to do the same. To suffer with dignity means not fearing what is happening to us or pretending that what life throws down before us does not touch us to the core. On the contrary, despite all that happens, it means that we do not allow fear to control us or permit suffering to overwhelm us. We embrace suffering as Jesus embraced the cross, trusting in God's benevolent care. Those who have faith believe that Jesus is with us in our suffering. Jesus' presence in our lives makes all the difference. He has gone before us in suffering and death, and accompanies us at every moment of our journey.

God does not cause suffering, but allows it so as to deepen our faith. Like any evil, suffering is a lack of something that should be there. Suffering was not a part of God's original plan of creation, but entered as an effect of humanity's primordial fall from grace. Most suffering is caused by human cruelty to each other and to the rest of creation. The human being is a microcosm of the universe. What goes on in the heart reverberates throughout the cosmos. The "sin of Adam" unleashed a downward spiral of hatred and violence. Jesus suffered and died to reverse that course. By uniting our suffering to Christ's, we contribute to that reversal in our own hearts and in the hearts of the people we touch. Jesus entered this world to end suffering and death. Although they are still with us, in the present moment Jesus uses them to deepen our trust in him.

God also uses suffering to test our faith. Scripture contains example after example of individuals being asked to sacrifice what was most precious in order to gauge the depths of their faith. Abraham's sacrifice of Isaac (Gn 22:1–19); Job's loss of wealth, family and health (Job 1–3); and Jesus' temptation in the wilderness (Mt 4:1–11) demonstrate how faith is purified in the forge of suffering. Using suffering for a higher purpose does not prove divine cruelty. God draws good out of all things (Rom 8:28) and never tests us more than we can bear (1 Cor 10:13). As Peter states in his first epistle, "even if now for a little while you have had to suffer various trials, so that the genuineness of your faith—being more precious than gold that, though perishable, is tested by fire—may be found to result in praise and glory and honor when Jesus Christ is revealed" (1 Pt 1:6–7). The closer we come to God, the more we see his hand in all things. He even uses human sins and failings to draw people closer to him than they ever dreamed. "O happy fault," the cantor at the Easter Vigil sings in the *Exsultet*.[16] Adam's sin gave God the opportunity to redeem humanity through the paschal mystery of his Son, not only restoring humanity to its former glory, but elevating it to new heights. God intends the same for our lives.

Suffering can also be an expression of love. Christ did not have to die on the cross to redeem the world. Being of infinite value, a single drop of blood or a single tear would have been enough to save not one, but a thousand worlds.[17] To show his love for us, Jesus *chose* the cross. Sacrificing self for another's sake demonstrates the deepest care and concern. Jesus himself said, "No one has greater love than this, to lay down one's life for one's friends" (Jn 15:13). Laying down our lives for others takes many forms: getting married, raising a family, becoming a priest or religious, dedicating oneself to community service, volunteering at a local charity, to name but a few. All are called to lay down their lives for their friends, and it is important to discern in the heart how God is asking us to do so. Each follower of Christ is called to emulate Jesus' selfless concern for others. As Jesus gave himself completely to the point of death, so must we place the needs of others before our own. We demonstrate our love for others in our willingness to undergo suffering without counting the cost, in particular the courage to suffer the hardships of the present moment (patience) and the ability to bear them on a daily basis (longsuffering).

Finally, those who are close to Christ not only embrace the cross, but also come to love it. They do so not out of some morbid delight in suffering, but because they love Christ and are deeply convinced of his love for them. Because of this intimate relationship, they love what Christ loved with all his heart and soul—the will of the Father. Jesus embraced the suffering of the cross because he believed giving up his life was the Father's way of showing unconditional love for humanity. Understanding how sacrificing one's only Son is an expression of love lies beyond human comprehension. It is impossible to comprehend the mind of God, but we can imagine that our willingness to give up a most prized possession or dearest relationship must resemble faintly what God is willing to do for his people. Jesus was so close to the Father that his death was like the Father losing a part of his own self. Jesus wants his love of the cross to become ours, because it reveals his Father's love for each of us.

Faith in Christ allows us to embrace the way of the cross, even to love it. Although the relationship between faith and suffering is far more profound than these few insights can hope to show, they suggest the path that every disciple of Christ must follow.

## Conclusion

Suffering touches everyone. It is part of the human condition, one of the realities of life. No one escapes its grasp. Try as we may to avoid it, at various points in our journey through life it awaits us. In my case, it meant being diagnosed in the prime of my life with a potentially deadly disease. Perhaps it has already taken its toll on you; perhaps your time is still to come. Suffering is not an illusion. We cannot wish it away or pretend it does not exist. We may—and should—try to alleviate its pain, yet we must learn to live with it, some for long, seemingly endless periods.

Dealing with suffering is the heart of the matter. On the most basic level, one that touches every aspect of our lives, each person must decide if suffering has meaning. On a purely human level, most would probably say, "Sometimes it does; sometimes it doesn't." Athletes, for example, put their bodies through intense, painful training in order to win. They strengthen themselves through discipline and hard work. People consider such suffering worthwhile, even admirable. The same holds true for dedicated scientists, artists, soldiers, scholars, students and everyone else who deny themselves for a greater good. On the other hand, what meaning is there in a small child dying of cancer, someone left homeless because of a fire, or a family left fatherless because of the carelessness of a drunk driver? Sometimes the suffering in the world is so overwhelming that it leaves us speechless.

Christian faith affirms that God has not remained silent before the ravages of human suffering. In the person of Jesus Christ, the Word of God himself became flesh, becoming like us in all things but sin (Heb 4:15). In his embrace of the cross he experienced the depths of human suffering, giving it new meaning through the power of his selfless love. In the world today, those who walk in his footsteps share in this redemptive suffering, witnessing to God's healing presence.

## Reflection Questions

✧ How do you deal with suffering? Do you ignore it? Do you pretend it does not exist? Do you try to grin and bear it? Do you accept it? Do you embrace it? Do you love it?

✧ Does faith enter the picture? If so, how?

✧ Do you believe that the different types of suffering require different responses? If so, how would you distinguish them?

✧ What do you think about Jesus' love of the cross? Do you understand the reasons behind it? How would you explain it to others? Do you believe his followers should express a similar love? Do you believe that ordinary believers can offer themselves in that way?

✧ Do you believe it is possible for a saint?

✧ Do you wish to follow the way of holiness?

✧ Do you desire to be a saint?

## Living Faith

Lord, help me to carry the cross of suffering.
Help me to bear it with courage and dignity.
Give me patience to suffer the inconveniences
of the present moment. Deepen my faith so I
can trust you in all things, in all times and in
all circumstances. Help me offer my suffering
up to you as an expression of your love for the
world. Renew my faith in sacrifice for a higher
cause, for the world's redemption. Help me to
see through my suffering and recognize it for
what it is. Help me to see your countenance
in the faces of those who suffer. Help me to
embrace them as you embraced your cross and
to love them as you loved the will of the Father.
*Mary, Mother of faith, pray for me.*

# 6

## Faith and Healing

As he went, the crowds pressed in on him. Now there was a woman who had been suffering from hemorrhages for twelve years; and though she had spent all she had on physicians, no one could cure her. She came up behind him and touched the fringe of his clothes, and immediately her hemorrhage stopped. Then Jesus asked, "Who touched me?" When all denied it, Peter said, "Master, the crowds surround you and press in on you." But Jesus said, "Someone touched me; for I noticed that power had gone out from me." When the woman saw that she could not remain hidden, she came trembling; and falling down before him, she declared in the presence of all the people why she had touched him, and how she had been immediately healed. He said to her, "Daughter, your faith has made you well; go in peace."

*Lk 8:42–48*

In the summer of 1979, when I was a seminarian, I was assigned to work in the Archdiocese of Philadelphia's healing ministry of the charismatic renewal, under the guidance of Br. Pancratius Boudreau, C.Ss.R. "Br. Panky," as we affectionately called him, was a pillar of the local charismatic community with a growing reputation as a faith healer. That summer I witnessed the effects of his prayer. After experiencing the deep, personal healing presence of the Holy Spirit in their lives, many found relief from or even a cure for their physical, emotional and spiritual distress.

The memories that stand out most are moments during a retreat or prayer service when he would process through the community with the Blessed Sacrament. As he passed, he asked people to touch the monstrance or, if they could not reach it, even the hem of his garment. In this way, he placed the Eucharist at the center of the healing event and helped those gathered to place themselves in the gospel story of the woman who had been suffering from hemorrhages for twelve years and was healed after touching the fringe of Jesus' garment as he passed (Lk 8:42–48).

Although some considered Br. Panky's practice unusual or even unorthodox, no one could dispute his creative way of making Word and Sacrament central to the healing experience. Taken together, his use of scripture and Eucharistic procession demonstrate the very heart of the Christian faith, living reminders that Jesus ministers throughout history in and through the community of believers.

## Jesus the Healer

In his day, the people knew Jesus to be a prophetic teacher and healer. In addition to offering the parables (Mt 13:1–3) and the beatitudes (Mt 5:1–12; Lk 6:20–23), he cast out demons (Mt 8:16–17), gave sight to the blind (Mt 9:27–31), hearing to the deaf (Mk 7:31–37), and speech to the mute (Mt 9:32–34). He made withered hands whole (Mk 3:1–6), the lame and the paralyzed walk (Mk 2:1–12), and the dead live again (Jn 11:1–44). He also exercised power over the elements of nature, turning water into wine (Jn 2:1–12), multiplying the loaves and fishes (Mk 6:30–44; 8:1–10), calming the raging sea (Lk 8:22–25). His powerful words demonstrated the in-breaking of God's kingdom among those who witnessed what he said and did.

His words could heal body and soul. Those he healed, moreover, often turned their lives around and followed him. Jesus stood in the long line of prophets like Elijah, Isaiah and Jeremiah who, when it was needed most, spoke God's challenging and consoling word to the chosen people. Such prophets presented God's message as a radical call to faith and repentance, summoning listeners to reform their lives and trust in God's benevolent care. Jesus' healings manifested his divine mission and the urgency of his redemptive message. He performed these acts not as ends in themselves, but as a foreshadowing of the ultimate healing of humanity's ills by his passion, death and resurrection.

Jesus' healing ministry, integral to his prophetic call, must be understood as part of his redemptive mission. He healed those who came to him not to display his power or to draw attention to himself, but to proclaim God's kingdom. The call to faith allowed his listeners to see the kingdom in their midst so the healing power of God could transform their lives. When his disciples asked him why they had not been able to cast out demons in his name, he told them simply, "Because of your little faith" (Mt 17: 20). For Jesus, faith and healing reinforce each other. Just as it did two millennia ago, his healing power manifests itself to the community of believers when they celebrate the sacraments and proclaim his Word.

## Healing in the Church

Although the Church, like Christ, is both human and divine, it will always need healing because, unlike Christ, it is sinful and therefore needs constant purification and renewal. *Lumen Gentium* states: "While Christ, holy, innocent and undefiled knew nothing of sin, but came to expiate only the sins of the people, the Church, embracing in its bosom sinners, at the same time holy and always in need of being purified, always follows the way of penance and renewal" (LG 8). Vatican II itself demonstrates renewal in the Church. From 1962 into the third millennium, it has provided a stable point of reference for the ongoing process of renewal in the Church, as demonstrated in the revised *Code of Canon Law* (1983), the *Catechism of the Catholic Church* (1992), and the twenty-five Synods of Bishops convened in Rome from 1967 to 2012.

Although the Church dispenses God's grace and its members seek holiness, they often fail to live up to the words they profess. Henri Nouwen describes the Church as a "wounded healer."[18] Even as it heals others, the Church itself needs healing on every level—the personal and the communal, the charismatic and the institutional, the priestly and the religious and lay states. Scandals involving the sexual abuse of children and financial indiscretions reveal the depths of the Church's wounds and its need for healing. The Church, a society of both saints and sinners, struggles between good and evil. This is the tension described in the Letter to the Romans: "[W]e know that the law is spiritual; but I am of the flesh, sold into slavery under sin. I do not understand my own actions. For I do not do what I want, but I do the very thing I hate" (Rom 7:14–15).

Healing is accomplished in the Church by the Holy Spirit, whose Pentecost gift to the community of believers brought forth a great outpouring of faith and the conversion, sanctification and healing of multitudes. The Spirit continues to heal through the Church's institutional and charismatic dimensions. *Lumen Gentium* affirms, "There is only one Spirit who, according to His own richness and the needs of the ministries, gives His different gifts for the welfare of the Church" (LG 7).

As an institution, the Church provides healing primarily through the sacraments, especially baptism, the sacrament of spiritual rebirth; Eucharist, the "medicine of immortality";[19] the forgiveness of sins in reconciliation; and the reinforcement of physical, mental, emotional, social

When Sheri Schiltz was nine years old, she embraced the gospel as a lifestyle and it became an integral part of her life. When she was eighteen, the first symptoms of leukemia emerged. The disease advanced rapidly, and she and her mother went to Seattle for a bone marrow transplant. She describes her experience:

*I was in a room with an older lady who had had the same transplant two weeks before. I noticed that the same ailments from the therapy would eventually reach me too. Then one day I learned that she had died. This scared me. But then I said "yes" to the will of God, and decided not to worry, sure of his love. Mom and I helped each other live moment by moment. Many times we had to renew our faith in the love of God, certain that he would take care of us.*

One day during a particularly rough moment, almost unable to speak because of the sores in her mouth, she heard her friends who had come to sing for her. In their act of love, she found new courage to face the pain. After that episode, the disease went into remission. Sheri reflected, *"Sometimes I feel overcome by the fear of a relapse, but each time I try to renew my 'yes' to God. I understand that none of us knows how long we will live. This experience has helped me to decide to live the gospel better than before."*

When the symptoms reappeared, she realized that she probably would not get better. She explained the impact this had on her relationship with God: *"Before I would pray to be healed. But now I understood that with this illness God wants to bring me closer to him. So now instead of praying only for physical health, I started to ask him, above all, for the grace to become closer to him."*

Sheri would not speak of her illness or of death, but of how she had lived. Her experiences were often as simple as picking something up off the floor for her mother, or how a medical visit had gone. After Sheri had passed away, many of her Catholic friends and family who had distanced themselves from their faith returned to the sacraments.[20]

and spiritual well-being in the anointing of the sick. The sacraments, an unbroken link with Christ's paschal mystery, transform every aspect of human life. The forgiveness of sins, the healing of illness and the conversion of hearts all point to the final healing of bodies, souls and spirits in the resurrection.

In the Church's charismatic dimension, the Spirit builds up its life, making Christ's healing and saving power present in the world by pouring forth gifts upon both individuals and groups such as religious orders and ecclesial communities. The sacraments and charismatic gifts are given to the Church for the good of the community, and in turn for the good of individuals and the world at large. They work together with prayer, charitable works such as the spiritual and corporal works of mercy, and ascetical practices such as fasting and abstinence to make present the kingdom of God and to renew the communion of saints on earth.

## Faith and Healing

The Holy Spirit accomplishes all healing in, with, and through Christ to give glory to God the Father. Although certain individuals are given a special gift of healing, God grants such gifts in order to demonstrate the power and truth of the gospel message. Faith in God can move mountains, can make all things possible (Mt 17:20; 19:26).

The sacraments, especially baptism, Eucharist, reconciliation and anointing of the sick are commonly called the "ordinary means of salvation." The term "ordinary" does not imply that these sacraments bring about only common or less miraculous healings. On the contrary, all sacraments point to the mystery of God's redemptive love and serve as instruments of grace that transform every aspect of human makeup. The sacraments are "ordinary" only in the sense that they are the usual means established by God for healing and for our ultimate transformation in Christ. Their results may seem less dramatic than other more spectacular healings because they reflect the humility of God and the abundance of the grace made available through Christ's paschal mystery. The sacraments are actions of Christ, visible signs of invisible grace given to heal and transform us so we might live in the Spirit through Christ in the presence of the Father.

Not only is the body healed, but every dimension of human makeup entrusted to God through faith. The deeper our faith, the more we rely on God's benevolent care for our physical, emotional, intellectual, spiritual and social well-being. Although those without explicit faith in God can and do experience healing, faith assists and at times even hastens the process. For example, the miraculous healing of a physical deformity or a fatal disease may not necessarily bypass the natural healing processes, but accelerate them. What might normally transpire over months or even years takes place in an instant. The same holds true for the other dimensions of human being. Since grace builds on nature, faith does not contravene the natural healing process, but completes and perfects it.

Healing, even for those without explicit faith, depends upon God's intervening love. Jesus did promise that whatever is asked for in faith will be received (Mt 21:22). God knows our deepest needs. If we ask for inappropriate gifts he will bestow not them, but only what is good for us at that moment (Mt 7:11). We petition God not so much to obtain a material good, but to understand his benevolent will and loving care. To pray with faith means to articulate our needs to God, trusting in his concern for our well-being without worrying whether specific requests are answered precisely as we framed them. Presuming that God will give us what we want just because we demand it of him manifests a lack of faith. An authentic relationship with God is based upon child-like trust, not childish manipulation. Mature faith brings to God all needs, large and small, trusting they will be fulfilled according to his will in a way that will help us to grow in virtue and holiness.

No matter the strength and depth of their faith, some receive healing and others do not. This seeming inconsistency can be explained not by our lack of faith or God's lack of love, but by his desire to use healing as a sign of the ongoing presence in the world of his redemptive love. Healing, in others words, is not an end in itself but an instrument that points beyond itself to life in the resurrection, where in a transformed existence all wounds will be healed and we will live in the presence of God. Those not healed in the present life demonstrate his redemptive love in another way, that is, by sharing in the passion and death of his Son. Uniting one's particular suffering with Christ's ultimate sacrifice contributes to healing the deep wounds of human nature brought about by Adam's fall from grace, ultimately freeing all human beings from the pangs of sin, ignorance, suffering and death itself. Although everyone will share in this suffering to some extent, God asks certain individuals to bear it in an intense and personal way. When it comes as it inevitably will, those closest to God praise him for this special sharing in Christ's paschal mystery.

Healing, on whatever level it takes place, is only a part of what God promises through the paschal mystery of his son. He wants not only to heal our wounds of sin and death, but also to elevate us to a new life in him. He wishes not only to make us whole, but also to draw us, fully alive with the life of his Spirit, into his presence. It is a mistake to consider the healing of our bodies, souls and spirits as the end of God's plan for our lives. Healing is only the beginning. God promises not only to restore us to health, but also to give us a new, transformed mode of existence, one that builds on human nature and transcends it. Jesus put it this way: "I do not call you servants any longer, because the servant does not know what the master is doing; but I have called you friends, because I have made known to you everything that I have heard from my Father" (Jn 15:15). Christ shares the intimate love of his Father and opens up the possibility of becoming God's children by adoption (Eph 1:5). The healing wrought by God's grace does much more than restore people to their original state of health. It promises to take them into the very presence of God and to offer them the riches of being his sons and daughters.

Finally, faith may make us whole, but the scars from the struggle remain. These marks serve as a vivid reminder of our ordeal and of the importance of relying at all times on God. Jesus provides the example par excellence of someone who in all things commends his life to God and whose suffering embeds itself in his very being. In his resurrected body Jesus retained the marks of his crucifixion, a visible reminder of his victory over suffering and triumph over death (Jn 20:24–29). The same holds true for all members of his mystical body. By uniting our suffering to Christ's paschal mystery we are healed, united to him in his transformed existence. Through faith, our suffering anticipates our healing and is remembered in the life to come. Faith and suffering are two aspects of a single mystery. Both, made possible by Christ's trust in the Father's love and the help he gives his followers to do the same, point to life in the resurrection.

Although this brief exploration of the connection between faith and healing does not exhaust the rich contours of the relationship, it does show how they interact and how they reflect the mystery of God's redemptive love. They also suggest how to view faith and healing not as ends in themselves but as a means to salvation, to being fully alive in the presence of God.

## Conclusion

Recalling my summer with Br. Panky, I am impressed not only by the way he linked the Word of God and the Eucharist with healing, but also by the confidence with which he prayed. This confidence was not a false, presumptive reliance on the strength of his own faith or that of the community of believers, but a trust founded deep in God's love and constant concern for each member of Christ's body. Panky prayed with confidence because he believed firmly that, no matter what happened, all those he prayed over would eventually be well—in life and in death. His confidence in prayer mirrors the words of the apostle James, "[A]sk in faith, never doubting, for the one who doubts is like a wave of the sea, driven and tossed by the wind; for the doubter, being double-minded and unstable in every way, must not expect to receive anything from the Lord" (Jas 1:6–8).

The relationship between faith and healing is as deep and mysterious as God's plan for the world's redemption. It centers on the Father's unconditional love; it takes Christ's paschal mystery as the deepest expression of that love; and in the Spirit it finds the way in which that love circulates among the members of Christ's body. This Trinitarian focus permeates the intimate relationship among faith, healing and everyone healed and transformed by the embrace of Christ's redeeming love.

Healing is never a private affair between God and the individual. It has a communitarian nature which, because of God's Trinitarian nature and because of Christ's redeeming love, continues through the members of his body, the Church. In the final analysis, all healing comes from God. In the natural order, it is he who makes our disordered bodily functions find their equilibrium and who, through the application of reason to the challenges that medicine confronts, guides scientists and doctors to discover and implement cures for disease. In the order of faith, it is he who heals through the Church's administration of the sacraments and who bestows charismatic gifts on individuals and faith communities for the good of Christ's body and of all humanity. God's love is self-diffusive. It refuses to contain itself and continues to pour itself out through the redemptive love of his Son.

## Reflection Questions

✧ How have you experienced healing? Has it been through instances of natural healing (recovering from the flu, a pulled muscle, a broken arm) or extraordinary, seemingly miraculous events?

✧ Have you ever experienced an emotional, psychological, or spiritual healing? If so, how did it differ from your experience of physical healing?

✧ Have you ever experienced healing on a communal level? If so, what stands out in your memory about that event?

✧ Have you experienced healing through the sacraments?

✧ Have you ever been healed through prayer and fasting?

✧ Why do you think these healings took place? What did they point to? How did they change you? Where does faith fit in, if at all?

✧ In which ways has God been present in your experiences of healing?

## Living Faith

Lord, I thank you for your healing presence in my life. When illness has struck me low and thrown me off balance, thank you for restoring me to health. Thank you for forgiving me my sins and restoring my spiritual health. Thank you for relieving me of my emotional and psychological anxieties. When I have departed from the community and lost my way, thank you for accepting me back. Thank you for my faith, which enables me to turn to you in prayer and bring to you my every need. Thank you for the sacraments, which mediate your healing, redemptive presence to the world. Thank you for the gift of healing that you have bestowed on communities and individuals to build up the Church. Thank you, Lord, for all your gifts. Let me never take them for granted. *Mary, Mother of faith, pray for me.*

# 7

## The Community of Faith

> Awe came upon everyone, because many
> wonders and signs were being done by the
> apostles. All who believed were together and
> had all things in common; they would sell
> their possessions and goods and distribute the
> proceeds to all, as any had need. Day by day, as
> they spent much time together in the temple,
> they broke bread at home and ate their food
> with glad and generous hearts, praising God
> and having the goodwill of all the people. And
> day by day the Lord added to their number
> those who were being saved.
>
> *Acts 2:43–47*

One of my most formative experiences during
college was membership in the Dartmouth
Christian Fellowship, an interdenominational
gathering of students trying to live a Christian
life at a secular university. Although we came from a wide
range of economic and cultural backgrounds, we were
united in our love for Jesus Christ and our intense desire
to walk the way of discipleship. This fellowship gave me a
strong ecumenical awareness and a deeper appreciation of
my own Catholic heritage, one that eventually led me to join
a religious congregation and become a priest.

Those of us in the Fellowship believed that Jesus Christ
wanted to be our most intimate friend and be present in
all we did. This personal relationship with Christ motivated
our every action. As with any friendship, we needed to work
at it by spending time in personal and group prayer and by

giving witness to Jesus' love through our words and deeds. Participating in the Fellowship led me to become a Big Brother; a leader in the Crusaders, a young boys' Christian fellowship; and a leader in the Catholic student organization known as Aquinas House.

The Fellowship emphasized the basics of the Christian faith, what C. S. Lewis refers to in his book of the same title as "Mere Christianity."[21] Typically, every Monday evening from seven to nine we met for fellowship in Rollins Chapel, then again during the week for an hour or so in smaller prayer groups at various locations around the campus. We were also encouraged to spend half an hour to an hour each day in personal "quiet time" with the Lord. In addition to these activities, we also went on weekend retreats and staffed a small twenty-four hour coffee house called *Agape*, where food and music were presented in a wholesome Christian atmosphere.

When I look back at that experience, I am most impressed with its strong sense of a community animated by a love for Jesus Christ, life in the Spirit and the desire to emulate the early Church's strong bonds of fellowship. These memories still support everything I do as a disciple of Christ.

## Fellowship in the Early Church

The Church came into being on Pentecost, when in a mighty wind and tongues of fire the Holy Spirit manifested itself to Jesus' followers and empowered them to convert thousands to the Good News of Jesus Christ (Acts 2: 1–13). These early disciples remained faithful to the teaching of the apostles, to their bond of fellowship (*koinonia*) and to the breaking of bread and the prayers. They sold their possessions and lived together, holding everything in common. Each day they went to the Temple for prayers, but gathered in their homes for the breaking of the bread. With generosity they shared their food and drink with each other, praising God in all things. The Lord added to their numbers day by day (Acts 2: 42–47).

Although Acts may present a somewhat idealized vision of the earliest Christian community, it does represent the life it aspired to and in many instances realized. In keeping with the Lord's teachings about the close connection between love of God and love of neighbor (Mt 22:34–40), the early Church dealt with tensions—between the rich and poor (1 Cor 11:17–22), Gentile and Jew (Gal 2:11–1), slave and free (Phlm 1:8–21)—in constructive and orderly ways. Their peaceful resolution generated a deep sense of unity in both the local and universal Church, inspired by the Spirit's presence and the ongoing guidance of the believing community. Throughout its history, whatever challenges that faced it, the Christian community has always sought faithfulness to the apostolic teaching, to life in communion and to the prayers. The Eucharist, moreover, has always remained central to its life, for it understood this celebration not as a mere commemoration of Jesus' Last Supper with his disciples, but as a living sacrament (*mysterion*) by which it touches the Risen Lord himself. This is the reality affirmed in the Second Vatican Council: "Really partaking of the body of the Lord in the breaking of the Eucharistic bread, we are taken up into communion with Him and with one another" (LG 7).

The Lord's presence in the Christian community lies at the heart of understanding its life and mission. In his first letter to the Church at Corinth, St. Paul describes this mystical presence using the analogy of the body: "For just as the body is one and has many members, and all the members of the body, though many, are one body, so it is with Christ. For in the one Spirit we were all baptized into one body—Jews or Greeks, slaves or free—and we were all made to drink of one Spirit" (1 Cor 12:12–13). Early Christians took this analogy seriously, for they believed that Christ was truly present in their community just as he was also present in the breaking of the bread. Their faith in the mystery of Christ's presence in their lives made them one in mind and heart, inspiring them to an apostolic mission of spreading the gospel message to every corner of the earth.

## Mystery, Communion, and Mission

The Second Vatican Council used three interconnected concepts to prepare the Church for a Second Pentecost: mystery, communion, and mission.[22] Rooted in Scripture and in the experience of the early Church, these concepts share a Trinitarian nature, Christological scope, and Pneumatic thrust. God, who is mystery, has revealed himself to the believing community as an intimate communion of love between the Father, Son and Holy Spirit, a love that pours itself out into the threefold mission of creation, redemption and sanctification. The Son of God became man so that human beings could share in this divine mystery of intimate communion and carry on his mission down through history and throughout the earth. Enlivened by the Spirit, faith puts Christians in touch with this mystery, calls them to community, sends them on mission.

The Holy Spirit then inspires a reverse process. Mission sends Christians back to the community, where they are nourished again by the living mystery of God present in their midst through proclaiming the Word and breaking the bread. To put it another way, celebration of the sacred mysteries, life in communion and apostolic mission are so deeply intertwined that they can be distinguished only in thought. Like intertwining strands of a single rope, the body of Christ is rooted in divine mystery, lives in divine communion, and is called to a divine mission. At every point, the Holy Spirit animates the community of the faithful as it takes up its cross to follow Jesus, the Son, in accordance with the Father's will. In this way, "the Church has been seen as 'a people made one with the unity of the Father, the Son and the Holy Spirit' " (LG 4).

To be Christian, a community must be grounded in this important spiritual triad. Without a strong focus on mystery, communion and mission, the body of believers loses its reason for being and begins to unravel. Although gaps between vision and reality have opened at various times in the life of the Church, the Spirit will never abandon it, seeking instead to close the breach by raising up inspired leaders and groups. Charismatic leaders like Benedict of Nursia, Francis of Assisi, Ignatius of Loyola, and John Paul II, along with religious orders like the Benedictines, Franciscans, the Jesuits, and the Vincentians, and, more recently, ecclesial movements like Focolare, Communion and Liberation, the Neocatechumenal Way and the Community of Sant'Egidio have served as leaven for the Church.

## Faith and Community

God has bestowed many blessings upon the community of the faithful, not the least of which are the institutional structures and charismatic gifts that give it order, longevity and vitality. These blessings are a work of the Holy Spirit, who imparts faith to the Christian community, transmits it to its members, and indwells their hearts. The relationship between faith and community has important consequences for Christian life.

Any discussion of Christian community must acknowledge the context of mystery, communion and mission that lies at the heart of its life and message. Although community is formed through human effort, it is not a mere collection of individuals with a similar outlook and interests, but a living spiritual organism that depends on and is sustained by its ongoing contact with the mystery of the Trinitarian God, made possible by the sacramental actions of Christ and a common life. Although Christian

*During her lifetime the founder of the Focolare Movement, Chiara Lubich, demonstrated what it means to live in a Trinitarian fashion. In this excerpt from a letter dated May 11, 1948, she conveys with passionate urgency what living the life of the Trinity on earth meant for her and her first companions.*

The Ideal we've embraced is God: Unity-Trinity and so it's as ineffable as infinite and eternal Love. And because of this, it's immanent, present (as God), even in the tiniest things, even in the smallest events!

God, Love, guides and does all things......

The important thing is to put unity at the beginning, the middle and the end. In this unity willed by God the two souls are melted into one, and they resurface equal and distinct. Just as in the most holy Trinity.

Jesus wants this in his Testament, which is the summary of everything he thought!

The thoughts of God!

"That they may all be one. As you, Father, are in me and I am in you." (Jn 17:21). What I mean to write to you today is that we must never break this unity that's been established by God.....

Maintaining yourself in unity, you'll begin to feel the strength of Jesus instead of your own strength; the Light of Jesus instead of yours; the love, the mercy of Jesus for every one of your neighbors, instead of your own.

And Jesus in you will be: "Love, that denial takes from none beloved . . ." that is, that infinite love that always wins out.

"Omnia vincit Amor," and the souls will be indissolubly linked to you, and they will bring you to God. Just so!

Because this is how God wants it.[23]

community takes many forms (family, parish, religious order, ecclesial movement—to name but a few) each is sustained by a life of faith that connects it with the divine mystery, calls it to fellowship, and strengthens it for mission. Faith is essential to every community's origin, formation and goals. Without faith, the community loses its identity and sense of purpose, succumbing easily to the forces of materialism and secularism that unravel its strong, intertwining unity and empty it of vitality.

Faith and community reinforce each other. An individual receives faith from God's people who, as a family of faith, initiate newborn children and catechumens through the sacraments of initiation: baptism, confirmation and Eucharist. Those individuals, in turn, are nurtured in faith through participation in the Church's sacramental life, ongoing catechesis, and love of the community expressed through family, friends, prayer groups, parish associations and similar gatherings. As they mature in faith, they give back through the community by participating more deeply in its call to mystery, communion and mission. In this light, faith is not a private possession but a gift God gives through the community and for the community's good. Inspired by this faith, each person is called by God to serve the body of Christ in a particular way. Although these calls share certain similarities, each serves the needs of the community in a unique way, fulfilling an irreplaceable role in the spiritual and temporal well-being of Christ's body, the Church.

The community of the faithful is a living, vibrant spiritual organism that translates vision into reality. Although it includes a system of imaginative and insightful teachings, Christian faith is much more than a collection of ideas concerning God and his Church to which believers give intellectual assent. It is a community sustained by a living faith and a palpable sense of God's presence in their lives. The Christian message seeks to flesh itself out in a living community that contributes to building up God's kingdom in a particular place and moment of human history. The community is incarnated as it comes to understand mystery, communion and mission. More than ideas to be formulated into a teaching and analyzed by experts, these concepts provide the guidelines for understanding how the Holy Spirit operates in a Christian community so that the Spirit's work of sanctification can be accomplished. The purpose and goal of the community of the faithful is holiness, a holiness born in the divine mystery, manifested by the community, and opened up to the world in mission.

Life in community buffers the relationship between the individual and the world, filtering social and cultural forces so that the constructive can be distinguished from the destructive. This interpretive function operates on many levels, providing the community as well as its individual members a way of discerning what is good and what is evil in the warp and woof of daily life. The Church's magisterium provides such guidance at local and universal levels; on a more particular level, religious orders, associations of the faithful and ecclesial movements are guided also by the collective wisdom of their constitutions and statutes. Each individual can find such guidance in the relationship of spiritual direction, whereby a well-trained director helps persons realize their identity in the faith. This interpretive role of the community enables individuals to navigate the challenging problems of the day and make prudent decisions based on scripture, the living tradition of the Church, the examination of conscience, and heartfelt prayer.

Building community, a work of the Spirit, also demands human effort. The Spirit manifests itself through the community's cooperation with grace and its response to the Spirit's promptings. Faith in God is manifested in actions that correspond with the gospel message, actions that are essential to maintaining the relationship with God as well as with neighbor. The author of the Letter of James states flatly that "faith by itself, if it has no works, is dead" (Jas 2:17). Faith verifies itself through action, and for Christians a primary work of faith is building community. Community is built when believers embrace a spirituality of unity that penetrates every aspect of their lives—the physical, the emotional, the intellectual, the spiritual, the social. Community is built when faith is incarnated in their own lives and in the lives of those they love. When they do so, faith becomes stronger and more capable of giving witness both within the community of the faithful and to the world at large.

Finally, in Christ's body faith depends upon a creative tension between the individual and the community. This tension preserves the rights, dignity and well-being of the individual while allowing the community to grow and develop in accordance with the common good. In its Trinitarian dimension, the Christian community seeks to avoid either extreme—isolation from the life of the community or its opposite, complete absorption by the community and an individual's consequent loss of identity. Maintaining a dynamic equilibrium between the needs of the individual and those of the community opens individuals to grow in all aspects of their lives, while the unique talents of each member enrich the community. This creative tension expands the horizons of faith for the individual and deepens the community's adherence to its gospel mandate.

Although much more can be said of the relationship between faith and community, these observations point to the bond they share and their mutual help for one another. Faith comes in and through community; building Christian community is very much a work of faith.

## Conclusion

Faith and community make the body of Christ live. The dynamic relationship between these elements enables the community of believers to continue its mission of proclaiming the Good News of God's love to the world and to live in the hope of one day seeing God face-to-face. Faith, hope and love—nourished and sustained in Christian community. The Apostle Paul asserts that the three things which last are faith, hope and love (1 Cor 13: 13). They are the common inheritance of God's People, who relate to God both as individual members and as a family.

My membership in the Dartmouth Christian Fellowship taught me a fundamental truth of the Christian life: we approach God as individual members of his body, each at various places along the path to holiness, and as a community of believers. Deciding to walk this path is personal, but also more communal than at first glance may be apparent. Believers are never alone on their pilgrimage of faith, for Jesus himself walks with them, leading his brothers and sisters into the presence of the Father. All along the way he encourages, guides, at times even carries them to their destination. The community is his, for his Spirit holds it together and animates it in carrying out his mission.

The Spirit animates the members of Christ's body, the Church, to bring God's creative, redemptive and sanctifying work to completion. The Spirit mediates God's presence to the world, for God, who is communal in nature, wishes to be a living presence in every human heart. Jesus himself said, "Where two or three are gathered in my name, I am there among them" (Mt 18:2). His presence in the Christian community distinguishes it from all other groups and gatherings. This presence is not the mere memory of a person or the recollection of a past event, but the presence of his own Spirit, who constitutes the Christian community as an organic, living reality. This living presence sustains the Church as it proclaims God's love for the world, affirms its faith in the crucified and risen Lord, and sheds its blood for the sake of the kingdom.

## Reflection Questions

✧ How have you experienced the Christian community? Which experience was most positive? Which was most negative?

✧ Have you felt indifferent toward community in any way?

✧ In your experience, how has the ideal of community life differed from its reality? If there were differences, were they large or small? Did the discrepancies grow larger or smaller over time?

✧ How can you tell when a community is dysfunctional? How can you tell when it is on the right track? Where does God fit in? Where does faith fit in?

✧ Is faith personal, communal, or some combination of both?

✧ How does the community impart faith to the individual? How does an individual reciprocate?

✧ How can community strike a balance between individuals' freedom and group identity?

✧ How does a community's life reflect its image of God?

## Living Faith

Lord, deepen my awareness of your presence in
my own life and in the life of my community.
Help me to sense your presence both within
my heart and in the midst of those gathered in
your name. Help me to contribute to the life of
my community so that I might give back what
I have received from it. Help me to find my
place in the community of believers. Give my
community the grace to be rooted in mystery,
communion and mission. Enable us to seek
you in all things and to proclaim your gospel
message boldly and fearlessly. Whatever we do,
Lord, may it be for you and for your kingdom.
Mediate your presence through us and help us
to draw others to you. *Mary, Mother of faith, pray
for us.*

# Conclusion

## Living the Faith
## in Today's World

"Lord, I believe; help my unbelief"

*Mk 9:19*

The Gospel of Mark includes the story of a man who pleads with Jesus to heal his son, mute since childhood and subject to violent epileptic fits caused by an unclean spirit. When told that his disciples were unable to cast the spirit out of the boy, Jesus exclaims, "You faithless generation, how much longer must I be among you?" (Mk 9:19). He then turns to the man and tells him that for those who believe all things can be done. The man, in turn, cries out "I believe; help my unbelief" (Mk 9:25). Moved by this response, Jesus heals the boy, giving him the possibility of leading a normal life among his family, friends and community.

In many ways, this man's story is our own. While facing the challenge of our own inner demons, we sometimes can only watch helplessly as the unclean spirits of ignorance, prejudice, hunger, war, deprivation, hatred and despair destroy members of the human family—even those closest to us. In this sense, Jesus' reference to his own "faithless generation" has relevance for us today. We say we believe, but struggle each day against the seemingly overwhelming forces of cynicism and unbelief. The secular world squeezes faith out of life and life out of faith, leaving a spiritual void filled by superstition, New Age spiritualism and interest in

94

the occult. Surrounded by hostile cultural influences, we must learn to live with the voices of doubt and uncertainty. Belief and unbelief vie to dominate our hearts. This struggle between spirit and flesh, light and darkness, life and death—a perennial theme in the Christian tradition—will not relent anytime soon.

How do we struggle against these worldly forces of chaos? For God's love to reign in our midst, we must affirm the good around us and distance ourselves from whatever hinders our life of faith. We must engage the world without compromising our core values. To prepare ourselves, however, we must align our own lives with true gospel values. What is more, we must do this together, as the body of Christ, a living community of faith with a clear purpose and mission. As stated in the Second Vatican Council's *Decree on the Church's Missionary Activity*, "The pilgrim Church is missionary by her very nature, since it is from the mission of the Son and the mission of the Holy Spirit that she draws her origin, in accordance with the decree of God the Father" (AG 2). In this light, the new evangelization is nothing less than the work of the Triune God to re-create, redeem and sanctify the human heart, human society and the whole created order.

We must begin this new evangelization with our own lives and move outward to family, friends, community, other levels of society and beyond. Once it takes root in our hearts, it can flow through us to others. Through it, we must console the world and challenge it to open itself to God's transforming love, thereby becoming better, a new creation. Through the new evangelization we must present the world with a living faith by which every person might become fully alive with the love of God and neighbor. That evangelization must be a faithful seeding by a faithful God in a soil prepared by grace and made fertile by prayer, fasting and almsgiving. What, then, does living the faith mean for those who seek to follow the way of discipleship?

**Conclusion One**: *Faith is not of our own making, but a response to a call.* Jesus of Nazareth calls us to follow him. When he walked this earth, he chose certain men and women to be his disciples. Today, he extends this call to everyone. To hear it, we must settle our hearts and listen to the still small voice within that asks us to trust God in all things. Through this trust, we enter into an intimate relationship with Christ and all that he shares with the Father.

*Reflection Questions*: Recollect the first time you experienced faith as a response to a call. Reconstruct the situation in your mind as clearly as you can.

- ✧ What people or events were involved in this experience? What were the first practical steps that you took in your walk of faith? Have you ever shared this experience with others? If not, why not?

- ✧ Put your experience down on paper. Be still before God and ask for the opportunity to share your response to this call with someone else.

**Conclusion Two**: *Faith is a gift from God.* It is not something we do, but something God does in us through the action of his Spirit. Many are offered the gift of faith, but receive it half-heartedly. We may say we believe in God and trust him with our lives, but our actions can tell a different story. To align our actions with our stated beliefs we need a change of heart (*metanoia*). Conversion of heart is a lifelong process. It too is a gift from God.

*Reflection Questions*: List everything for which you are grateful. Be as specific as possible. Include material things, but also relationships with family members and friends. Include also any spiritual gifts you have received, such as your capacity to listen and understand or your capacity to love.

- ✧ Where does faith fit in? Do you view it as a gift? If so, have you opened that gift and used it to your fullest capacity? Have you thanked God for it? Have you thanked those who have shared their faith with you?

**Conclusion Three**: *Faith is not a blind embrace of the absurd, but a recognition of our limits in understanding the mystery of life.* Faith does not contradict reason, but complements and even elevates it. There is not a truth of reason and a truth of faith. Truth is one, although it may be approached from different perspectives. Some have narrowed reason to include only that which can be verified empirically. Doing so, however, impoverishes and even distorts reason. Reason can learn from faith—and faith from reason.

*Reflection Questions*:

✦ How would you explain why you believe in God to someone who does not believe?

✦ Can you demonstrate that your belief in God is not an irrational leap into the absurd, but a rational conclusion drawn from your experience of life? What images or metaphors might you use in your explanation?

✦ How would you describe the relationship between faith and reason?

✦ How would you reconcile faith with reason?

✦ How would you respond to an atheist's unbelief? In what sense is this unbelief also an act of faith?

**Conclusion Four**: *Faith is a seed that needs to be carefully tended.* Prayer is the life-giving water that nourishes the gift we receive at baptism, helping it grow to maturity. We nurture our faith by fostering a healthy prayer life. The deeper our life of prayer, the more we will trust God in all things. Faith and prayer need each other. We cannot pray without faith.

Without prayer, faith shrivels and dies. Taken together, faith and prayer enable us to walk the path of holiness.

*Reflection Questions:*

- ✧ How has prayer deepened your life of faith?
- ✧ Has prayer increased your knowledge about God or deepened your knowledge of God? What is the difference between these two kinds of knowledge? Has prayer helped you in both areas?

Think of all who have accompanied you in your walk of faith. Think of all who have prayed that you grow in your relationship with God. You may wish to list all who have helped you deepen your trust in God. Pray for each of them—one by one. Thank God for their presence in your life. Thank God for the gift of prayer.

**Conclusion Five**: *Faith gives meaning to suffering.* Without faith, suffering is aimless, without purpose. With faith, we can let go of our suffering, knowing that a loving, caring, benevolent God will bring good out of our ordeal. Christ's death on the cross shows that God is not indifferent to human suffering, but deeply involved in it. Through faith, we can unite our suffering with Christ's and share in God's redemptive plan for humanity.

*Reflection Questions:*

- ✧ How have you suffered in your life?
- ✧ What crosses have you been asked to carry? How have you managed them? What has helped you get through the day? How has your relationship with Christ helped you?

On pieces of paper write all of your hardships, old and new, and tack them to a cross or crucifix. Keep in close view this reminder of the connection between your sufferings and Christ's. Whenever you look at it, turn to God in prayer and ask him for the strength to carry on.

**Conclusion Six**: *Faith brings about healing on all human levels—the physical, the emotional, the intellectual, the spiritual and the communal.* Belief in the resurrection assures us that one day we will experience the fullness of life in every area of human experience. It is a mistake, however, to use faith to test God or to reject sound medical practice. True faith means trusting God in all things. In this life, people of strong faith are sometimes healed of their illnesses—and sometimes not. Miracles of faith manifest God's power and point to the love he holds for each person.

*Reflection Questions*:

- ✧ What healings have you experienced? On which level of your human makeup have they taken place? Have they come about by natural means or through supernatural intervention?

- ✧ What is the deepest possible healing a person can undergo?

- ✧ Have you ever received healing in answer to your prayers?

- ✧ Have you ever asked God to heal someone else? If so, how has God answered those prayers?

- ✧ What healing do you need at this moment in your life?

- ✧ Have you placed your needs in God's hands?

Be still and ask God to lead you to intercede for those who need your prayers.

**Conclusion Seven**: *Faith is both personal and communal.* Faith in Christ sustains the community and the individuals that comprise it. The community of faith sustains even those who lead solitary, contemplative lives. Those who follow Christ must participate in the sacramental and devotional life of the Church in order to be true disciples. Their call has two essential dimensions—to communion and to faith. Faith calls us into community with fellow believers and with all humanity. Life in community, in turn, deepens faith and helps us to continue Christ's work on earth.

*Reflection Questions:*

♦ With which community of faith do you identify most closely: your family, a prayer group, your local parish, a religious order, an ecclesial movement? Why do you identify with it so much? What are its strengths and weaknesses? How can you help this particular faith community grow even closer to God? How does this community relate to other faith communities? How does it relate to the universal Church? How does it relate to non-Christian communities of faith? How does it relate to non-believers?

♦ Where do you see gaps between vision and reality in your faith community? What steps can you take to bridge these gaps?

The Second Vatican Council reminds us, "[F]aith throws a new light on everything, manifests God's design for man's total vocation, and thus directs the mind to solutions which are fully human" (GS 11). Elsewhere, the council affirms: "The Word of the Lord is compared to a seed which is sown in a field; those who hear the Word with faith and become part of the little flock of Christ, have received the Kingdom itself. Then, by its own power the seed sprouts and grows until harvest time" (LG 5). The seed of faith benefits all who yearn for the coming of the kingdom. It can be viewed from many perspectives, and is one of the three things that last (1 Cor 13:13). It gives us new birth and is a leaven for the world around us. It renews human nature and elevates it. It can change hearts, personal relationships, families, communities, societies and the world at large. To reach its full effect, however, its power must be harnessed and then unleashed in creative life-giving ways.

Faith is not a weapon, but a way of being that encourages people to trust in the benevolent care of a loving God. It takes in intellect, will and emotion. It speaks to the heart and pours itself into our entire being. It is a mustard seed in need of careful tending in the garden of our hearts, yet it can unleash the transforming power of God in the community of the faithful, one heart at a time. It provides eyes to see and ears to hear. It helps us befriend God and, through the power of Christ's paschal mystery, become his adopted children. It enables us to walk the path of holiness. It gives us "the assurance of things hoped for, the conviction of things not seen" (Heb 11:1). It helps us to focus on the one thing that matters. It inspires us to give glory, praise and honor to God in all we think, say and do. It is a treasure for the community and for the individual. It places its hope in Jesus, "the way, the truth, and the life" (Jn 1:6). It brings us into the presence of the Father. It makes us members of the body of Christ, humble servants of those in need, temples of the Holy Spirit. It is the most precious gift, one that carries us beyond suffering, beyond life, beyond death—to the peace and tranquility of our eternal home.

# Acknowledgements

All quotations from Scripture come from *Holy Bible: The New Revised Standard Version with Apocrypha* (New York, Oxford: Oxford University Press, 1989). Part of Chapter Two has appeared elsewhere under the following title: "The Star of Bethlehem: Our Search for the Living God," *Liguorian* 99 (10, 2011): 8–12. Part of Chapter Three has appeared elsewhere under the following title: "The Unfolding of a Tradition," in *Spirituality and Morality: Integrating Prayer and Action*, Dennis J. Billy and Donna Orsuto, eds. (Mahwah, NJ: Paulist Press, 1996): 9–31. A special word of thanks goes to Gary Brandl, Tom Masters, Jim Webber, and Julie James of New City Press for their invaluable help at every stage in the evaluation, preparation, marketing, and distribution of this book.

# Notes

1   Official Church documents tend to use the words "man" or "men" to signify human beings as a group.

2   See, for example, Avery Dulles, *The Assurance of Things Hoped For: A Theology of Christian Faith* (New York: Oxford University Press, 1994); H. Richard Niebuhr, *Christ and Culture* (New York: Harper & Row, 1951); Paul Tillich, *Dynamics of Faith* (New York: Harper & Row, 1957).

3   Excerpt from the story of "Madeleine," in Thomas Masters and Amy Uelmen, *Focolare: Living a Spirituality of Unity in the United States* (Hyde Park, NY: New City Press, 2011), 54–55.

4   Athanasius, *De incarnatione*, 54.3 [SCh 199:458–59; PG 25:191–92]; Gregory of Nyssa, *De opificio hominis*, 16 [SCh 6:151–61; PG 44:178–88].

5   O. Henry, "The Gift of the Magi" (1906). Available at *The Literature Network:* http://www.online-literature.com/donne/1014/.

6   Lisa Ernstberger, "My Life in the Focolare," *Living City* (April 2004), 5.

7   http://www.vanityfair.com/culture/features/2010/09/hitchens-201009.

8   See, for example, Alasdair MacIntyre, *Whose Justice? Which Rationality* (Notre Dame, IN: University of Notre Dame Press, 1988), 349–69.

9   See Frederick Copleston, *A History of Philosophy*, vol. 3, *Augustine to Scotus* (Garden City, New York: Image Books, 1985), 441.

10  See Frederick Copleston, *A History of Philosophy*, vol. 7, *Fichte to Nietzsche* (Garden City, New York: Image Books, 1985), 343–46.

11  Augustine, *Confessions*, 1.1, trans. Rex Warner (New York: New American Library, 1963), 17.

12    See Anselm of Canterbury, *Proslogion*, 1 in *Anselmi opera omnia*, ed. F. S. Schmitt, vol. 1 (Stuttgart: Friedrich Frommann, 1984), 100.

13    See Frederick Copleston, *A History of Philosophy*, vol. 4, *Descartes to Leibnitz* (Garden City, New York: Image Books, 1985), 169–73.

14    Tom and Mary Hartmann, *Gifts from Heaven: Providence in Our Family* (Hyde Park, NY: New City Press, 2012), 80–82.

15    From Thomas Masters and Amy Uelmen, *Focolare: Living a Spirituality of Unity in the United States* (Hyde Park, NY: New City Press, 2011), 132–33.

16    See *The Roman Missal*, 3rd ed (Magnificat, 2011), 338.

17    See Alphonsus de Liguori, *Dignity and Duties of the Priest or Selva* in *The Complete Ascetical Works of Saint Alphonsus de Liguori*, vol. 12 (Brooklyn, NY: Redemptorist Fathers, 1927), 26.

18    Henri J. M. Nouwen, *The Wounded Healer: Ministry in Contemporary Society* (New York: Image Books, 1979).

19    See, for example, Ignatius of Antioch, *Letter to the Ephesians*, 20.1 in *Early Christian Fathers, ed. Cyril C. Richardson* (New York: Macmillan, 1970), 93.

20    Excerpted from Thomas Masters and Amy Uelmen, Focolare: Living a Spirituality of Unity in the United States (Hyde Park NY: New City Press, 2011), 176–78.

21    C.S. Lewis, *Mere Christianity* (San Francisco: Harper Collins, 2001).

22    See, for example, LG 1, 4, 7– 8, 12, 17, 25–27, 33–36; DV 8; GS 1; AG 5,28; CD 2–16.

23    Chiara Lubich, *Early Letters: At the Origins of a New Spirituality* (Hyde Park, NY: New City Press, 2012), 108.